T0341950

Global Finance

Leo Gough

FINANCE

05.02

- ■ Fast track route to mastering global finance and macreconomics

- ■ Covers the key areas of global finance, from the theory of comparative advantage and the aims of the WTO/GATT to multinational business and managing forex risk

- ■ Examples and lessons from some of the world's most successful businesses, including Ford, NTT DoCoMo and Nestlé, and ideas from the smartest thinkers, including Paul Romer, Milton Friedman, J M Keynes, Paul Krugman and Alan Greenspan

- ■ Includes a glossary of key concepts and a comprehensive resources guide

>>EXPRESS EXEC.COM<<
essential management thinking at your fingertips

First published 2002 by
Capstone Publishing (a Wiley company)
8 Newtec Place
Magdalen Road
Oxford OX4 1RE
United Kingdom
http://www.capstoneideas.com

CIP catalogue records for this book are available from the British Library and the US Library of Congress

ISBN 1-84112-203-3

This book is printed on acid-free paper

Substantial discounts on bulk quantities of Capstone books are available to corporations, professional associations and other organizations. Please contact Capstone for more details on +44 (0)1865 798 623 or (fax) +44 (0)1865 240 941 or (e-mail) info@wiley-capstone.co.uk

Contents

Introduction to ExpressExec

ExpressExec is 3 million words of the latest management thinking compiled into 10 modules. Each module contains 10 individual titles forming a comprehensive resource of current business practice written by leading practitioners in their field. From brand management to balanced scorecard, ExpressExec enables you to grasp the key concepts behind each subject and implement the theory immediately. Each of the 100 titles is available in print and electronic formats.

Through the ExpressExec.com Website you will discover that you can access the complete resource in a number of ways:

» printed books or e-books;
» e-content – PDF or XML (for licensed syndication) adding value to an intranet or Internet site;
» a corporate e-learning/knowledge management solution providing a cost-effective platform for developing skills and sharing knowledge within an organization;
» bespoke delivery – tailored solutions to solve your need.

Why not visit www.expressexec.com and register for free key management briefings, a monthly newsletter and interactive skills checklists. Share your ideas about ExpressExec and your thoughts about business today.

Please contact elound@wiley-capstone.co.uk for more information.

Introduction

Lower barriers to the flow of goods, labor, and capital is bringing about a globalization in finance and business generally. This chapter considers the causes of the process.

» The rationale for globalization.

"Tariff: A scale of taxes on imports, designed to protect the domestic producer against the greed of his consumer."

Ambrose Bierce[1]

In 1994 billionaire businessman the late Sir James Goldsmith published a book called *The Trap* in which he argued that what is wrong with the trend towards the greater internationalization of trade is that industries in developing countries are paying lower wages than their competitors in the West.[2]

People have been making this celebrated error, known as the "pauper labor" fallacy, for nearly two hundred years. What is curious is that Goldsmith, a highly successful entrepreneur by any standards, should be arguing against free trade in such terms.

As we will see throughout this book, the globalization process is all about reducing barriers to the free movement of capital, goods, and labor between all the countries of the world. Most governments are, with some reservations, broadly in favor of the process, as are most economists, because they believe that lowering these barriers will boost world growth – by co-operating, everyone will get richer. In this view, richer countries need to be constantly moving into industries where they have an advantage, such as high technology, allowing less developed nations to develop and export. Low wages in a Third World country, they say, are a function of low productivity in that country's industry. If that industry becomes highly productive, wage rates will rise. Singapore and Japan, for example, today enjoy comparable wages and living standards to the West because of their success in building productive industries over the last 40 years.

Economic growth is not a zero-sum game. If Country A is rich, this does not mean that Country B has to be poor. The more productive the world is, the richer it gets as a whole – and working to distribute wealth to all people is part of the process of increasing productivity.

A way to make everyone richer? Why would any business person be against the idea? Perhaps this is not as odd as it seems. Businesses are primarily interested in their own profits. A company may be able to make excellent profits in a country where everyone else is doing badly; working for the general good is irrelevant to the central business goal. Also, it takes decades, at least, for a country to become prosperous, while businesses have to focus on making profits in a much shorter period.

This book is about how macroeconomic events are affecting businesses everywhere. Most of the time, companies must focus on microeconomic issues – events in their markets, their industries, their supply chain, and so on. When the underlying structure of the world economy changes, as it is today, companies have to take notice; the opportunities are immense, but so are the dangers.

The availability of cheaper capital in the global markets, a reduction in labor bargaining power, the rise of imports, the increase in cross-border mergers and acquisitions, the opening up of huge markets such as China and India, changes in public attitudes, demographic change, and the e-revolution are just some of the factors in globalization. They are not going to go away, and companies that ignore them or fail to understand the underlying reasons why they are occurring, are being acquired or going out of business.

In Europe, for instance, Siemens has reduced its operating divisions from 15 to 5, as has Thyssen Krupp (from 23 to 8), Fiat's Agnelli family has sold 20% of the firm to General Motors, Daimler-Chrysler has purchased US company Chrysler and UK company Vodafone made the first hostile takeover ever to take place in Germany when it acquired Mannesmann.

Everywhere you look in the world, globalization is having an effect. It is probably having a financial impact on your company already. If not, it soon will.

NOTES

1 Bierce, A. (2000) *The Unabridged Devil's Dictionary*. University of Georgia Press.
2 Goldsmith, J. (1994) *The Trap*. Macmillan, London.

What is Global Finance?

This chapter introduces five basic concepts in global finance and examines the role of international business.

» Macroeconomics
» The theory of comparative advantage
» Growth
» Types of economic system
» Ways of classifying economies
» International business.

"every individual ... endeavors as much as he can ... to direct ... industry so that its produce may be of the greatest value ... He intends only his own gain, and he is in this, as in many other cases, led by an invisible hand to promote an end that was no part of his intention .... By pursuing his own interest he frequently promotes that of society more effectually than when he really intends to promote it ."

Adam Smith

In this chapter we will look at some commonly used ideas in macro-economics and international business.

MACROECONOMICS

Macroeconomics is the study of whole economies, as opposed to "microeconomics," which looks at how individual industries, house-holds, and businesses function. While macroeconomics is a vital concern of governments, it is also essential to businesses, espe-cially those with operations overseas. Macroeconomic concerns, such as currency exchange, inflation, unemployment levels, economic development, and international trade, are a major element in success-fully managing operations in a complex and ever-changing environment.

THE THEORY OF COMPARATIVE ADVANTAGE

One of the most important ideas in economics is comparative advan-tage, originally propounded by David Ricardo, a British economist and politician of the early 1800s. The proposition is simply that nations, societies, and members of those societies collectively benefit most by specializing in what they do best, even if some parties are "absolutely" more efficient producers than others.

To follow the argument, imagine two people, A and B, on a desert island, who have only two jobs to do: collecting coconuts and fishing. Assume that they agree that both items are of equal value – 1 coconut is worth 1 fish. Person A is better than Person B at both tasks (see Table 2.1).

The problem is to decide how A and B should spend their time.

Table 2.1 Productivity per day worked.

	Coconuts	Fish
Person A	20	20
Person B	10	16

A could tell B, "You are a bad worker, so stay out of my way and do nothing." The result of this would be a maximum production capacity of either 20 coconuts or 20 fish per day.

B may be a less productive worker, but he can still make a contribution. To find the most productive way of dividing their labor, they look at the "opportunity cost" of the alternatives (see Table 2.2).

Table 2.2 Opportunity cost.

	Produced	Opportunity cost
When A collects coconuts	20 coconuts	20 fish not caught
When B collects coconuts	10 coconuts	16 fish not caught
When A catches fish	20 fish	20 coconuts not collected
When B catches fish	16 fish	10 coconuts not collected

A and B need both coconuts and fish. If A catches fish and B collects coconuts, they will produce 20 fish and 10 coconuts per day, but if A collects coconuts and B catches fish, they will produce 16 fish and 20 coconuts.

Since they both agree that 1 coconut is worth 1 fish, they will collectively produce more units of value (36) if A collects coconuts and B collects fish than if they divide their labor the other way around (30 units of value).

In economic jargon, A has an "absolute" advantage in both coconut and fish production. B, however, has a "comparative" advantage in producing fish since he can produce 16 units of value per day for an opportunity cost of only 10 units of value.

GROWTH

Every day we are exposed to the notion that growth is very important and we could be forgiven for wondering why. While there may be philosophical differences over the true value of growth (some people may prefer to live simply, while others want everything they can get), many misunderstandings arise because of confusion over the concept of economic growth.

Economic growth is the increase in the total production output of an economy. As long as output grows faster than the population, the standard of living increases. Economic growth happens when an economy either finds new resources or when it finds ways of producing more using existing resources. Since the Industrial Revolution that began around 250 years or so, much of the world has done both. The population has increased dramatically (see Table 2.3), yet living standards have, overall, gone up.

Table 2.3 Increasing agricultural production (corn and wheat) in the US: 1939–1995. (Source: US Department of Agriculture Statistics, 1992; Statistical Abstract of the United States, 1996.)

Year	Corn		Wheat	
	Yield per Acre (BU)	Labor hours per 100 BU	Yield per Acre (BU)	Labor hours per 100 BU
1939	26.1	108	13.2	67
1949	36.1	53	16.9	34
1959	48.7	20	22.3	17
1969	78.5	7	27.5	11
1979	95.3	4	31.3	9
1985	107.2	3	36.9	7
1990	112.8	NA	38.0	NA
1995	120.6	NA	38.1	NA

In developed countries, agricultural productivity has greatly improved. For example, in the US, the productivity in corn and wheat have grown massively since the 1930s, while the work needed to produce it has dropped by over 90% (Fig. 2.1).

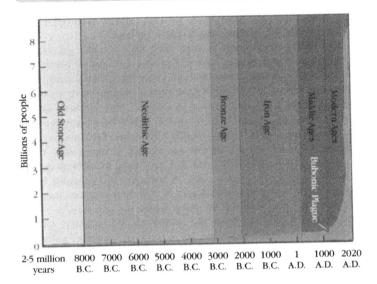

Fig. 2.1 World Population Growth.

This extraordinary improvement has been achieved by advances in scientific knowledge, farming equipment, and farming techniques, none of which could have developed without the investment of money and labor through successive generations.

Today, poorer countries face difficulties in achieving growth. Growth comes in many ways, but the two most important drivers are technological advance and accumulating capital (in the sense of useful assets such as roads, factories, and machinery). Both of these drivers require investment, and poor countries have trouble in diverting resources from producing essentials, such as food and clothing, into projects that will create long-term growth.

TYPES OF ECONOMIC SYSTEM

In practice, most countries have a "mixed" economic system, where there is both government involvement and a degree of freedom in the markets. In their pure form, there are two extreme possibilities: the command economy and the laissez-faire economy.

The command economy is controlled by a central government that owns state enterprises, and sets production targets, prices, and incomes. In recent years, command economies have not done well – the economies of the former USSR and Eastern Europe have collapsed and undertaken a painful transition to a market economy with varying degrees of success. While countries such as Poland have been recording real growth since 1992, others, such as Albania and Romania, have not enjoyed much foreign investment and remain in dire straits. China has undertaken a series of reforms that have freed its markets dramatically – some cities in China, such as Shanghai, are capitalist boom towns – while retaining a large degree of government involvement.

The "pure" laissez-faire economy is where the government has no participation at all. Individuals and companies buy, produce, and sell as they wish, and the outcomes are a result of countless individual decisions. Supporters of free market systems argue that they encourage efficiency, because an inefficient producer will be driven out by better competitors, and that the consumers have great power because businesses will respond to their demands. Prices will adjust themselves automatically as supply and demand fluctuates.

Laissez-faire has problems too, however. It can be demonstrated that inefficiencies can and do exist. Without government involvement there can be many injustices, and it is a feature of laissez-faire that there are recurrent episodes of unemployment and inflation.

Although most economists agree that some government intervention is desirable, there is a perennial debate about how, and how far, it should go (see Chapter 8).

WAYS OF CLASSIFYING ECONOMIES

There are nearly 200 sovereign states in the world, each with its own economy. The International Monetary Fund (IMF), the United Nations (UN), and the World Bank all have different ways of classifying the world's economies, reflecting these organizations' own agendas.

The most widely used system in business is the IMF's, which classifies nations into three groups:

» *industrial economies*: the 23 most industrialized countries, including the US, Canada, Japan, Western Europe, Australia, and New Zealand;
» *developing countries*: some 130 nations in Latin America, Asia, the Middle East, and Africa. Some countries in this group have enjoyed substantial growth in recent years, so there is now a subcategory of "newly industrializing countries" (NICs) including such powerhouses as Hong Kong, Singapore, South Korea, and Taiwan;
» *transitional economies*: 28 countries of the former Soviet bloc that are now trying to develop market economies.

INTERNATIONAL BUSINESS

International trade had always been important, but during the last 20 years countries have become markedly more interdependent. A widespread restructuring of economies to adapt to freer trade and capital movements, and in response to the collapse of the USSR, is occurring. While this presents many new opportunities for business, it is by no means certain that the process is irreversible. As we will see throughout this book, there are many forces and issues that are directly or indirectly resistant to globalization. Although some believe that multinational companies (MNCs) are a major factor in driving further globalization, others argue that MNCs are actually much more closely tied to their countries of origin than is generally appreciated, and that they tend to pursue national, rather than global, objectives (see Chapter 9, *The Myth of the Global Corporation*). There are also worries that globalization could increase the wealth gap between rich and poor nations.

KEY LEARNING POINTS

» While microeconomics looks at the "trees" of units such as individual businesses and households, macroeconomics looks at the "forest" of a whole economy.
» The theory of comparative advantage is the essential argument for free trade – it states that free trade benefits all partners, even those who are "absolutely" more efficient.

» Economic growth is defined as the increase in the total production output of an economy.

» "Command" economies are run by the government, which sets prices, production levels, and wages. In laissez-faire economies, the government does not interfere in market processes. In the real world, all countries have some degree of government participation in their economies.

» The IMF groups countries into three economic categories:
  1 industrialized (includes the US, Western Europe, and Japan);
  2 developing (the rest of the world);
  3 transitional (the ex-Soviet Bloc countries).

» International business has greatly increased over the last 20 years. "Globalization" is the great business issue of the day - but no-one knows how far it will go or how long it will last.

The Evolution of Global Finance

How did we get here? From Adam Smith and David Ricardo to twentieth century attempts to manage increasing economic complexity. How multinationals evolved.

- » The evolution of macroeconomics
- » The evolution of multinationals
- » The General Agreement on Tariffs and Trade (GATT) and the World Trade Organization (WTO)
- » GATT – the Uruguay round
- » The International Monetary System (IMS)
- » Timeline: Key events in the development of global trade and finance.

"Without stable political foundations, markets collapse."

Doremus et al.[1]

The most important and long-lived controversy in macroeconomics is the debate over free trade (see Chapter 8) – how much, or little, should governments interfere in business? In 1776 Adam Smith made the then revolutionary claim that the market system, in which everybody competes for selfish gain, actually results in more benefits for all people than a directed system. His famous assertion, quoted at the beginning of Chapter 2, that an individual working for their own gain is "led by an invisible hand to promote an end that was no part of his intention," has become one of chief tenets of market-based economies.

In the early 1800s, British landowners controlled Parliament; import and export of grain had been controlled by the Corn Laws, a collection of tariffs, subsidies, and restrictions intended to reduce imports, boost exports, and keep the price of grain high. Newly wealthy factory owners emerged wanting cheap food so that they could keep the wages they paid low. The debate lasted for years, resulting in the eventual repeal of the Corn Laws in 1848.

The British economist David Ricardo supported repeal and developed the argument for free trade that still remains the central point today: that specialization and free trade will benefit all trading parties, even when some are "absolutely" more efficient producers than others.

THE EVOLUTION OF MACROECONOMICS

Although the term "macroeconomics" was not coined until after the Second World War, the Depression of the 1930s marks its birth as a practically applicable body of ideas. During the 1930s, international trade slumped and there were rounds of "competitive" currency devaluations as countries tried to make their export goods cheaper. Traditional theorists believed that wages would drop to a level where there was little unemployment, but for a decade unemployment across the world remained high. John Maynard Keynes, a British academic, developed a solution, arguing that what was needed was for governments to intervene and stimulate overall demand.

Following the end of the Second World War, Keynes' ideas gained wide acceptance and governments increasingly used taxation, public spending, and intervention in interest rate levels and the money supply to try to manage their economies.

By the 1960s, confidence in governments' ability to keep economies stable was at its height; many people believed that it was possible to "fine tune" the economy to control variations in production output and employment levels.

In the 1970s, following the oil crisis of 1973 when the OPEC oil-producing nations dramatically increased prices, the developed nations experienced wild fluctuations in inflation, unemployment, and production output. The new phenomenon of "stagflation" appeared, where a rapid price inflation combined with high unemployment – prior to the 1970s, inflation had only occurred during periods of prosperity and low or declining unemployment.

By the 1980s, it was clear that "Keynesian" economics as generally understood was not working effectively. Criticisms ranged from the simple argument that government bureaucracies were not efficient enough to act quickly to more complex theoretical views that cast doubt over whether monetary and fiscal policies could actually affect the overall economy at all.

Monetarism (see Chapter 8) generally favors a slow, steady increase to the money supply in line with growth in output and is against governments actively trying to influence the economy by expanding the money supply during bad times and slowing the growth in the money supply during good times. In the 1970s, the debate between monetarist and Keynesian approaches was a huge controversy as governments struggled to cope with inflation and unemployment.

Two other macroeconomic approaches developed out of the chaos of the 1970s, "new classical" economics and "supply-side" economics. New classical economics suggests that people and businesses have rational expectations about the economy and that government intervention can have little effect on overall output – it advocates very little government intervention. Supply-side economics focuses on the idea that heavy regulation and high taxation reduces incentives to be productive (work, save, and invest). Deregulate and reduce tax, they say, and the economy will expand. During Ronald Reagan's presidency in the 1980s, the US experimented with supply-side ideas. Did they work? The jury is still out, with supply-siders pointing to the facts that after tax cuts in 1981 the US recession ended, federal receipts rose throughout the 1980s despite the tax cuts, and inflation fell during the period. Opponents counter that the national debt increased by $2trn between 1983 and 1992 and argue that higher tax rates would not have dampened economic growth.

Today, there is still much disagreement over the competing macroeconomic theories. They are difficult to test conclusively because there is not enough data – the half century since WWII is simply too short a period of time. The different theories are also difficult to standardize in ways that allow them to be tested against one another. In short, macroeconomics is still a young science and there is much left to learn.

THE EVOLUTION OF MULTINATIONALS

Although multinationals appeared in the early 1800s it was not until the 1870s that MNCs developed in a form that we would recognize today. Technological developments and organizational innovations allowed the creation of vast global enterprises, most of which were based in Europe. Some of these, such as British American Tobacco, Nestlé and Michelin, are still major corporations today. In the late nineteenth century, these MNCs were principally focused on gaining control of commodities in the colonies with which to supply products at home and for export. They were not yet a major force on the business scene, however, with much international business being dominated by cartels.

MNCs came into their own after WWII. US firms entered foreign markets in force, but concentrated mainly on developed countries, rather than on the raw material producers of the prewar era. US MNCs employed large numbers of skilled workers, advertised massively, and had intensive R&D programs.

By the 1970s, MNCs began to change as Japanese and European companies began to flex their muscles. Japanese firms began to use newly industrialized countries (NICs) as "export platforms" for their products while European companies entered the US market and increased their ownership of US firms. As a result of the rapid growth of newly industrialized countries since 1980, a new generation of multinational firms have appeared in Asia (in particular, from Taiwan, Singapore, Hong Kong, and South Korea) and to a lesser extent in Latin America.

Today, MNCs are major players in world business, with their foreign affiliates accounting for about a third of total world gross domestic product (GDP).

THE GENERAL AGREEMENT ON TARIFFS AND TRADE (GATT) AND THE WORLD TRADE ORGANIZATION (WTO)

GATT was originally signed in 1947 by 23 industrialized nations including the US, the UK, France, and Canada. In 1995 it was succeeded by the WTO. GATT has had eight rounds of international trade negotiations, all aimed at reducing trade barriers. In the grim post-war atmosphere of 1947, the average import tariff in industrialized countries was around 40%. Today it is around 5%. In the 1960s, the "Kennedy" round of GATT achieved an average cut of around 30%, reducing manufacturers' costs by about 10% by 1972. In the late 1970s, the "Tokyo" round also achieved tariff cuts of approximately a third, with greater cuts for trade between the most developed countries and smaller cuts for trade between developed and newly industrialized countries.

As well as addressing tariffs, GATT also tries to reduce trade discrimination by insisting that any trade advantage given to one member country must be given to all other members. Exceptions are allowed for free trade areas and customs unions such as the European Union.

GATT – THE URUGUAY ROUND

The most recent completed round of multinational trade negotiations began in Uruguay in 1986 and was finally concluded in Geneva in 1993, although the US did not approve it until 1994. It is the biggest and most comprehensive trade agreement ever made, and its supporters claim that it will increase the volume of international trade of merchandise by 9–24% over what could otherwise be achieved.

The three most significant features of the Uruguay round are:

1 Tariffs and protections for agriculture are reduced. Historically, agriculture has often been the most protected of industries. Uruguay

calls for an average reduction of agricultural tariffs on imports of 37%.

2 Uruguay bans restrictions on the import of services such as banking, insurance, computer consulting, legal services, and accounting.

3 Increased protections for intellectual property. Local laws usually protect domestic intellectual property, such as copyrights, patents, and artistic works, but internationally "piracy" is common. Uruguay requires its signatories to protect foreign owners of intellectual property to the same degree as they protect their own.

A major criticism of GATT is that it lacks teeth; compliance is voluntary. Developed countries have generally complied with GATT agreements, but there have been numerous cases where some have not. A disagreement between the EU and the US in the early 1990s over oilseed subsidies resulted in the EU refusing to comply with some GATT recommendations for several years and only capitulating when the US threatened to impose tariffs in retaliation.

The WTO is intended to solve this problem by a streamlined disputes system with binding arbitration; more than half of the disputes brought so far have been between the US and the EU.

THE INTERNATIONAL MONETARY SYSTEM (IMS)

1870–1914

Gold had been used as a store of value for millennia, but by the late nineteenth century world trade had increased so much that there was a need for a more sophisticated system of a more formalized system of settling international trade accounts. Countries began to set their currency at a certain value relative to gold and the "gold standard" became the accepted international monetary system within Western Europe in the 1870s, with the US adopting it in 1879.

It was a period of low inflation, and the "rules of the game" were clear. Every country set the rate at which its currency could be converted to gold. For example, sterling was pegged at £4.2474 per ounce of gold while the US dollar was pegged at $20.67 per ounce. The pound/dollar exchange rate was therefore calculated as shown in the equation below:

$$20.67/4.2474 = 4.8665$$

$$£1 = \$4.8865$$

Each country promised to give anyone gold in return for its currency on demand, so maintaining adequate reserves of gold was vital. A major effect was to limit the rate of growth in the money supply to the rate at which a country could acquire additional gold.

1914–1944

With the outbreak of the First World War, everything changed. The gold standard was abandoned and currencies were allowed to fluctuate over wide ranges. Speculation against weak currencies and in favor of strong ones helped to cause exchanges rates to become far more volatile than was justified by the "real" values of currencies; and companies were unable to offset these changes in the forward exchange market because it was then relatively thinly traded. In the inter-war years this had the effect of preventing world trade from growing proportionately with the growth of world gross national product (GNP). In the Great Depression of the 1930s, world trade declined to very low levels.

By the mid-thirties, cash was no longer convertible to gold except by central banks. With the outbreak of the Second World War, many of the main trading currencies could not be exchanged for other currencies and by the end of the war only the US dollar remained as an easily-exchanged currency.

Bretton Woods 1944

The Allies of the Second World War met at Bretton Woods in New Hampshire in 1944 to discuss how to create exchange rate stability once the war had ended. Since the United States had become by far the most powerful country in the world, it was agreed that the new international monetary system would be based on the US dollar, with every currency being given a fixed exchange rate to the dollar. The system itself was tied to the US dollar at $33 to an ounce of gold.

The World Bank and the International Monetary Fund (IMF) were created; the World Bank assisted reconstruction after the war and subsequently provided aid for economic development, and the IMF serves as a lender of last resort for central banks in countries that are experiencing difficulties with exchange and balance of payments; its principal purpose is to help keep the system relatively stable. During the 1990s, the IMF has played a significant role in assisting countries such as Russia, Brazil, Mexico, Thailand, and South Korea during financial crises.

1945–1971

For nearly two decades, the dollar-based system worked well, as countries worldwide struggled to rebuild their economies and world trade grew rapidly.

If a country wished to change its exchange rate, it had to make a formal announcement that it was revaluing, or devaluing, its currency. In 1949, 28 countries devalued their currencies.

Bretton Woods set the stage for the rise of socialism. Countries were able to pay for the huge cost of creating welfare states by issuing bonds, which in turn encouraged inflation. As world trade mushroomed and the economic balance between countries began to change, vast funds grew up which were highly mobile and could be switched from one country to another without the permission of governments. The demand for gold was high, and the official price of $33 to an ounce was undermined by the creation of secondary markets, where gold was traded at much higher prices.

Large dollar funds developed outside the US, which created a lack of confidence in the dollar/gold value. In 1971, the US gold reserves were reduced by a third in the first seven months and President Nixon suspended official gold transactions. This was, in effect, a unilateral decision to abandon the Bretton Woods system and the world's currencies were allowed to "float" in relation to the dollar. By the end of the year, most of the major trading currencies had appreciated against the dollar. A second dollar devaluation of the dollar occurred in 1973 when it fell to $42.22 per ounce, a drop of 10%. By June 1973 it had fallen by another 10%.

1973–today

In a floating exchange rate system, no currency is formally linked to any other, or to gold. The rate at which you can exchange one currency for another is simply the best rate that someone will give you, so exchange rates are highly volatile. During the oil crises of 1973 and 1979, when OPEC dramatically increased the price of oil, the floating system helped to minimize the chaos as the strain was taken by an adjustment in exchange rates (the OPEC countries' currencies suddenly became much more valuable), rather than by stopping real economic activity.

Today, there are diverse ways of controlling exchange rates – some countries allow their currencies to float freely with the market, while others "peg" their currency to fluctuate within a fixed range against the dollar. Overall, the current system is best described as "managed floating," with nations' central banks intervening in currency markets occasionally to try to influence their exchange rates.

TIMELINE: KEY EVENTS IN THE DEVELOPMENT OF GLOBAL TRADE AND FINANCE

- » **1848**: The protectionist Corn Laws repealed in Britain, a landmark victory for free trade.
- » **1870s**: Multinational companies, such as Nestlé and Michelin, develop to exploit new technical processes.
- » **1914**: The First World War forces countries to abandon the gold standard. Exchange rates fluctuate wildly, to the detriment of world trade.
- » **1930s**: The Great Depression – mass unemployment and a dramatic slowdown in international trade casts doubt on the idea that free markets are fully self-adjusting. J.M. Keynes argues that governments can stimulate economies by spending.
- » **1944**: The Allied powers meet at Bretton Woods to devise a system for stabilizing exchange rates and promoting growth and trade. All currencies are tied to the US dollar, and the IMF and World Bank are created.
- » **1947**: The GATT trade agreement, intended to reduce international trade barriers, is signed by 23 nations.
- » **1950s**: American MNCs grow rapidly in developed foreign markets, investing heavily in R&D and using sophisticated marketing methods.
- » **1971**: The US abandons the Bretton Woods system, and currencies are allowed to float against one another.

» **1973**: The OPEC oil cartel hikes the price of crude oil, throwing the developed world into recession.
» **1970s**: Stagflation (high inflation and unemployment) appears. European and Japanese firms grow to become MNCs. Keynesian ideas are challenged by monetarism.
» **1980s**: New classical economics and supply-side economics increase in influence. Growth, especially in Asia, encourages a new generation of MNCs to emerge from the newly industrialized countries (NICs).
» **1993**: The Uruguay round of GATT is concluded.
» **1990s**: Globalization and free markets are in the ascendancy, with countries all around the world privatizing state-owned firms and reducing barriers to free capital flows.
» **1995**: GATT is succeeded by the World Trade Organization (WTO).
» **2000**: A preliminary meeting of the WTO to discuss a new trade round in Seattle collapses amid recriminations between developing countries, the US and the EC, while outside there are violent protests. An anti-globalization movement gathers strength (see Chapter 6).

KEY LEARNING POINTS

The Industrial Revolution brought massive opportunities for growth, and a fierce debate over the relative benefits of free trade versus protectionism developed that is still raging today.

The inability of governments to deal with the problems of the Great Depression of the 1930s gave rise to Keynesianism, which encourages state intervention to stimulate demand.

The end of WWII ushered in a new era of prosperity and stability based on Keynesian principles and a new international monetary system linked to the US dollar. GATT was established to work towards lowering trade barriers around the world and to encourage trade.

Since the 1950s, multinational companies have increased in importance. Multinational companies first arose in America, then in Europe and Japan, and finally in the NICs such as South Korea. Today, MNCs are major players in world business, with their foreign affiliates accounting for about a third of total world gross domestic product (GDP).

Oil shocks, stagflation, and public sector inefficiencies in the 1970s gave rise to new approaches to managing the economy, in particular monetarism, new classical economics, and supply-side economics. Today, controversies still remain over which, if any, of these approaches provide accurate models of how the world really works.

NOTE

1 Doremus, P.N., Keller, W.W., Pauly, L.W. & Reich, S. (1999) *The Myth of the Global Corporation*. Princeton University Press, Princeton N.J.

The E-Dimension

Looking at the Internet as part of a continuum of IT advances. Ideas about the effects of technological advance on growth. What's new about the New Economy?

» Is there really a New Economy?
» Best practice? Changes in the forex business.

". . . suppose that, for whatever reason, the market goes up month after month; your MBA-honed intellect may say 'Gosh, those P/Es look pretty unreasonable', but your prehistoric programming is shrieking "Me want mammoth meat!" – and those instincts are hard to deny."

Paul Krugman, economist

IBM chief Lou Gerstner said in 1999 that the booming dot-com companies were just "fireflies before the storm." A real boom is coming, he thinks, when "the thousands and thousands of institutions that exist today seize the power of this global computing and communications infrastructure and use it to transform themselves."

The Internet can be seen as part of a continuum of IT advances that are leading to a networked world where the physical cost of communications is virtually zero. This is likely to transform the supply chains of big businesses, saving billions of dollars by slashing processing costs, procurement cycles, and the prices of purchases. Major car companies such as Ford and Chrysler are already claiming huge savings through e-business. Ford's parts division Visteon (now spun off as a separate company) serves small dealers via the Internet, producing large efficiency gains. Ford is also developing business-to-consumer e-applications that promise the public more personalized cars.

On the level of individual companies and industries, e-business clearly offers opportunities to beat the competition through more efficient communications. But what will this mean overall during the next two or three decades? One possibility is that it will accelerate outsourcing so much that large companies will split up into loose alliances of smaller units and independent knowledge workers.

A change in the way corporations are organized looks likely. What is less clear is whether the elimination of the cost of communications will really have a substantial effect on the growth rates of the developed world – as envisioned by the "New Economy" pundits.

IS THERE REALLY A NEW ECONOMY?

Stanford economics professor Paul Romer (see Chapter 8) has an amusing way of looking at the limits to growth: the total amount of matter and energy in the universe remains the same, and what human beings do when they produce things is rearrange some of that matter. The better we get at finding "recipes" for rearranging matter, the more productive we are – for example, by making previously worthless silicon into silicon chips for computers.

Romer is optimistic about the potential for new discoveries to sustain or increase growth rates in the future. He points to the recent discovery of superconductive materials that may ultimately have economically dramatic applications, and argues that just to evaluate all possible unknown combinations of the known elements in the periodic table in search of new "recipes" would take an unimaginably long time with existing techniques. The scope for future discovery, therefore, is vast, says Romer.

Paul Romer is a respected economist who is one of the authors of "New Growth Theory" which emphasizes the importance of knowledge and discovery in the economy (see Chapter 8). Romer believes that the per capita GDP is highest in the US now because the US invested more than other countries in knowledge and discovery during the twentieth century. In other words, the US is reaping the rewards in growth terms for its investment in innovation.

So far, so good. The idea that technological innovation is economically very important is not new. In 1957, for instance, the economist Robert Solow calculated that about 90% of the increase in per capita GDP in the US in the first half of the twentieth century was due to technological advances.

In the 1990s, however, enthusiasts began to claim that the extraordinary success in the US of the knowledge industries (including information technology, the Internet, biotechnology, and telecommunications) combined with international financial liberalization and trade growth, were creating a "New Economic Paradigm." In the "New Economy," they said, US workers have become much more productive, doubling the country's potential growth rate and lowering unemployment without a corresponding increase in inflation. Productivity growth has accelerated and the official statistics that do not support this are failing to measure the New Economy accurately. Most traditional economists think that measures of productivity have in any case understated the improvement in living standards for more than a century.

In 1997, the US economy looked particularly good, with 4% GDP growth (against an average of 2.4% annually over the previous two decades), inflation under 2%, and unemployment at a 25-year low of 4.6%. Between 1995 and mid-1998, American households increased their net worth from stock market gains of some $6trn. Since then, the collapse of the dot-com stocks, a down-turn in the overall stock market and a looming recession has called much of the New Economy optimism into doubt. The rules of the "Old Economy" may not have been repealed after all.

There can be little doubt that high-tech advances have brought about productivity gains on a microeconomic level (see below), but the New Economy rhetoric is making macro, not micro, claims. What is remarkable about it is how rapidly the idea of a New Economy has been taken up in business. Serious businesspeople have been taking the New Economy seriously; why? On a micro level, it is not hard to understand – your business may or may not be able to gain advantages by entering e-commerce, say, and at the very least you need to understand what all the fuss is about. Most business is done at the microeconomic level, so why should the New Economy's macro claims matter? The answer could be simply that it is good for business confidence. The hope of increased growth is an attractive one; we all like to feel that everything is getting better in a general way, and if our customers, suppliers and investors think so too, so much the better.

In Chapter 4 of *Finance Express* (also in the ExpressExec series), the potential microeconomic effects of the New Economy are discussed in detail. Here we are examining the New Economy's two principal macroeconomic claims:

» that in the late 1990s the US economy, despite the low official figures, was actually experiencing high productivity growth;
» that expanding demand will not lead to inflation, even if unemployment is very low. Global competition will prevent US firms from raising their prices.

The first claim, of high productivity growth, looks a little shakier in late 2001 than it did during the late 1990s. The OECD latest provisional GDP forecasts predict US growth of 1.1% for 2001 and 1.3% for 2002, with similarly low figures for other leading countries and actual shrinkage in Japan: -0.7% for 2001 and −0.8% for 2002.[1]

How unusually good was 1997? Not that unusual – in 1983, for instance, growth was almost 7% without a change in inflation, but growth dropped to a lower rate over the next 10 years (an average of 2.4%). The economy fluctuates, and there are sometimes short-term increases in output, particularly following a period of underuse of capacity. In 1982, the US economy was in recession, with high unemployment, and 1983's growth surge could be accounted for by the process of taking up the slack in the labor force.

Economist Arthur Okun proposed the "law" that unemployment decreases by 1% for every 3% increase in GDP. Although subsequent research has shown that this relationship is less stable than he supposed, as a rule of thumb it seems to demonstrate that the higher-than-average growth in both 1983 and 1997 could be explained by the drops in unemployment in those years (2.2% in 1983, 0.6% in 1997).

But why has inflation remained low? Until recently it was generally thought that if US unemployment fell below about 6% inflation would rise as workers, knowing that they were in a seller's market, demanded higher wages. The answer could be that other factors have helped to keep inflation low: the Asian financial crisis of 1997 reduced costs of imports to the US, for instance. It is possible that the "sustainable" unemployment rate at a steady inflation rate has dropped a little, perhaps due in part to a more flexible labor market and a fear of downsizing. If the low inflation rate can be explained by slow growth in wages and employee benefits, it is not evidence for the new invisible boom in productivity claimed by New Economy apologists.

While recognizing that such low inflation during a period of business expansion was puzzling, Alan Greenspan, Chairman of the Federal Reserve, had to this say about this issue in late 1998:

"Some of those who advocate a 'new economy' attribute it generally to technological innovations and breakthroughs in global-ization that raise productivity and proffer new capacity on demand and that have, accordingly, removed pricing power from the world's producers on a more lasting basis.

"There is, clearly, an element of truth in this proposition. In the United States, for example, a technologically driven decline is evident in the average lead times on the purchase of new capital equipment that has kept capacity utilization at moderate levels and virtually eliminated most of the goods shortages and bottlenecks that were prevalent in earlier periods of sustained strong economic growth.

"But ... as the first cut at the question "Is there a new economy?" the answer in a more profound sense is no. As in the past, our advanced economy is primarily driven by how human psychology molds the value system that drives a competitive market economy."

Alan Greenspan[2]

Greenspan went on to argue that developed economies are always changing and evolving, in general towards a more efficient system – we have been upgrading and modernizing constantly since the start of the Industrial Revolution. He agrees with the New Economists and others that most of the growth in output has been created by the application of new ideas, and suggests that our tendency to make things smaller (transistors, microprocessors) may be linked to the increased costs of processing more and more physical resources.

Like all scientists, economists tend to talk about probabilities, not certainties. Greenspan and others think that it is probable that there is no "New Economy" in any lasting sense. An excellent period of growth does not necessarily mean that fluctuations in confidence, inflation, employment, investment, and so on have permanently ended.

BEST PRACTICE? CHANGES IN THE FOREX BUSINESS

The world's biggest financial market is foreign exchange, where an estimated $1.5trn changes hands every day. The wholesale end of the market, dominated by banks, has always been cut-throat. Currency brokers and traders operate on tiny margins to execute customer orders for foreign currency – as little as 0.002% of the value of the transaction.

Banks have been using bespoke electronic networks for many years for forex trading between themselves, which made them slower to adopt the Internet than other financial markets, such as stocks and bonds. Having their own network kept up their margins; corporate customers would typically telephone their bank to ask for an exchange rate quotation and there were limits to how far companies could compare rates between different banks. Retail customers are even further removed from the market, paying as much as 5% to purchase small amounts of foreign currencies from banks and money changers, with hotels often charging even higher rates.

Now the foreign exchange market is moving to the Internet. Major US and European banks have formed consortiums to offer e-forex services to companies. Chase, Citibank and Deutsche Bank (who together control 28% of the global forex market) have partnered with Reuters, the information services provider, to form Atriax. Another 70 second-tier banks have joined them. Atriax competes with FXalliance, a consortium of 13 other major international banks that controls about 31% of the market, including Credit Suisse First Boston, Goldman, Sachs Group, HSBC Holdings, JP Morgan, Morgan Stanley Dean Witter, and UBS Warburg.

Philip Weisberg, of FXall, says that "the liquidity and market leadership that will be provided by FXall's member banks provide clients with greater price transparency, tighter pricing, and quicker order execution than is currently available offline."

The new trading platforms bring this antiquated market into the modern era. Atriax's boss Dan Morehead said: "The [forex] industry is fairly antiquated. People still make phone calls, scurrying from one bank to another to get prices. The industry does not even have a centralized marketplace, let alone an electronic one." Celent, a banking consulting firm, predicts that by 2004 at least 50% of all forex trading will be over the Internet.

Widespread job losses have already occurred as telephone-based "barrow boy" forex traders find that their limited skills are no longer required. Much online trading is automated, meaning the demise of the majority of the back-office accounting staff as well.

Margins are likely to continue shrink as the disintermediation process accelerates. Independently owned multi-bank sites, such as

Currenex.com, are offering new forex services to companies, such as the ability to trade on their own. There are even schemes to offer retail customers forex trading, such as OANDA.com.

Banks are under threat from these new competitors. The challenge for them is to find innovative ways to keep the business for themselves. One promising strategy is the cross-bank R&D alliances that are forming to develop cutting-edge technology for e-banking services. By sharing a "killer app" across the whole industry, banks might be able to fend off outsiders in the long term.

KEY LEARNING POINTS

- The Internet "disintermediates" (cuts out middle men) and drives down prices because of "price transparency" (you can compare prices more easily) and efficiency gains.
- The physical cost of communications is dropping massively. Large companies are enjoying major savings by putting their supply chains online. Ultimately this could lead to a devolution of companies into loose networks of small, independently owned units.
- "Knowledge," in the sense of technological advances, is generally recognized to have been the main engine for growth in developed countries during the twentieth century. The US, Japan, and Europe are all roughly at the same level of technological development - the US may be ahead in microprocessors, for instance, but Europe is ahead in mobile telephony.
- A period of strong US growth in the 1990s fuelled by knowledge-based industries gave rise to claims that there was a "New Economy" or a "New Economic Paradigm" of accelerating productivity growth without more inflation. Some argued that the productivity of the new businesses were being underestimated in official growth figures and that this was evidence that the limit to US growth without unacceptable inflation had changed. This argument is questioned by traditionalists who say that standard productivity measures have always underestimated productivity because no one has found a way to measure the total effects of innovations (the car, antibiotics, etc.) - we do

not know whether or how the unmeasured part of productivity growth has changed.

» The idea that the US economy will grow faster in the future than it has in the past is an attractive one to almost everyone in business everywhere. Faster US growth suggests more sales, more investment, more entrepreneurial opportunities, more stock market flotations, and so on worldwide. The idea of the New Economy spread rapidly, perhaps because it supplies a rationale for business confidence about the future.

» The claim that productivity growth would continue to accelerate indefinitely is challenged by a worldwide economic downturn beginning in 2000/01. There seems to be little evidence that the familiar phenomenon of economic booms and recessions has ended. To judge whether knowledge industries really boosted productivity growth starting in the 1990s, we will have to wait several decades to see the overall trend.

NOTES

1 *Financial Times*, October 19, 2001.
2 Alan Greenspan, speaking at the Haas Annual Business Faculty Research Dialogue, University of California, Berkeley, California, September 4, 1998.

The Global Dimension

The power of multinationals (MNCs) and the advantages of becoming one, particularly in finance. Governments' attitudes towards MNCs.

» Variety in NIC companies – the Ultraman battle
» Why become an MNC?
» MNCs vs governments
» Technology alliances
» The financing of MNCs
» Best practice: Novo.

"If states are understood ... as institutional structures or polities, then the basic institutional structure of transnationals will be influenced or even determined by the institutional characteristics of states."

Stephen Krasner[1]

The United Nations estimated in 1998 that there were 53,607 multinational corporations (MNCs) with some 448,917 affiliated companies. The total sales of foreign MNC affiliates actually far exceed the world's exports and amount to around a third of total world GDP.

It is often said that the largest multinationals have GDPs bigger than small countries; it's true. In fact, half of the largest economic units in the world are multinationals, not countries, measured by turnover or GDP. Only 14 nations have larger GDPs than the largest MNCs (see Table 5.1).

Table 5.1 The top 10 multinationals by foreign assets. (Source: UNCTAD, 1998.).

Ranking by Foreign Assets	Country	Currency	Industry
1	General Electric	US	Electronics
2	Shell, Royal Dutch	UK/Neth	Petroleum
3	Ford Motor Company	US	Automotive
4	Exxon Corp	US	Petroleum
5	General Motors	US	Automotive
6	IBM	US	Computers
7	Toyota	Japan	Automotive
8	Volkswagen Group	Germany	Automotive
9	Mitsubishi Corp	Japan	Diversified
10	Mobile Corp	US	Petroleum

As we saw in Chapter 3, until the 1980s, most MNC activity occurred in the developed countries, with around 50% of production occurring in the US, UK, Canada, Germany, and Holland, but the dynamism of the newly industrialized countries (NICs) has created a host of young home-grown multinationals, particularly in Asia. Until the 1990s, the world's trade was dominated by North America and Europe, but East Asia is now a powerful third force; together, the three trading areas account for the vast majority of MNC activity, about 1/3 of world exports and around 60% of manufacturing output.

VARIETY IN NIC COMPANIES – THE ULTRAMAN BATTLE

Many Westerners tend to think of Asian business as almost wholly based on heavy manufacturing and information technology, driven by state-run central planning; but less earthy businesses are increasingly common. As an illustration, here is an example of a recent court battle between a Japanese and a Thai company over the intellectual property rights for a cartoon character.

Ultraman, a popular cartoon character from Asia, originally appeared in comics in the 1940s. A 1960s television series featuring the superhero was sold widely across the world. In 2001, Tsuburaya Productions of Japan sued Chaiyo Production in Thailand alleging unauthorized reproduction of Ultraman images and claiming 100 million baht (£1.6mn) in damages. Chaiyo's boss, Sompote Sangduenchai, argued that he had originally proposed the Ultraman character to Tsuburaya's late founder, Eiji Tsuburaya, and that it was inspired by images of traditional Thai buddhas. He also claimed that Tsuburaya granted Chaiyo the rights to produce Ultraman movies worldwide outside Japan in return for financial assistance given in the early 1970s. The character has evolved substantially over the years, and the case, Thailand's highest profile intellectual property dispute of the year, revolves around the definition of Ultraman – Tsuburaya claims the present character was not designed until 1966.

WHY BECOME AN MNC?

Although the largest MNCs are concentrated in the oil, automotive, and electronics industries, MNCs overall are in a very wide variety of businesses. Most economists think that the principal motive for extending a company's reach beyond its home ground is the search for higher and/or more stable profits over the long term, either by increasing sales or reducing costs.

Cost-focused MNCs tend to grow internationally by buying suppliers ("vertical integration") in the hope of cheaper raw materials or a more secure supply. The classic example is the major oil companies who set up long-term extraction arrangements around the world after the end of the First World War to ensure their supply of crude oil. In the 1980s and 1990s many manufacturers in the developed world set up assembly plants in areas such as South-East Asia and China, often exporting parts for assembly and then reimporting them into their own countries for sale. The developing world offers an abundance of high quality labor in countries that do not demand substantial additional payments beyond wages paid for work done, unlike the developed world, where non-wage elements (such as social security contributions) range from 50%–80% of the total in many countries.

Market-focused MNCs tend to spread "horizontally," seeking new markets in other regions. While long range forecasts are notoriously inaccurate, many, including the World Bank, believe that by 2020 markets such as China and India will be larger than those of most developed countries today (see Fig. 5.1), and many MNCs are seeking to establish their presence in these promising areas.

MNCS VS. GOVERNMENTS

The staggering scale of MNC operations causes unease amongst governments, particularly those of poorer nations, for a number of reasons.

One is the effect on the balance of payments. A foreign MNC may bring capital into the country, in which case there is an initial gain, or it may borrow or raise equity locally. Ultimately, however, the MNC hopes to repatriate far more profits than the amount it invests, negatively affecting the balance of payments.

Another difficulty is the so-called "Trojan Horse" effect. Western European countries with high unemployment have tried to create jobs by encouraging foreign multinationals to set up business. Efficient MNCs that have done so have been criticized because they have outcompeted less efficient domestic rivals, thus causing job losses. A variation on this theme is some EU member states' fears that non-EU MNCs invited into

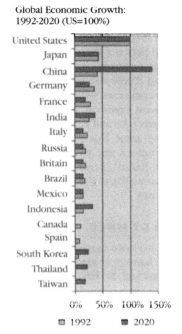

Global Economic Growth:
1992-2020 (US=100%)

Fig. 5.1   Projected global economic growth.

the UK will have a Trojan Horse effect in France, Germany, and Italy as their cheaper/better products are exported within the EU.

By their nature MNCs have far more opportunities for efficient tax planning than one-country firms, despite numerous regulatory efforts on the part of governments (see the book *Finance Express* in this series).

TECHNOLOGY ALLIANCES

In the 1970s, MNCs co-operated on developing technology by forming separate corporate entities which they owned jointly with their partners. This pattern shifted during the 1980s towards informal alliances which they organize together to reduce R&D risks and costs – in general, it works best when the partners have different sets of expertise. Between 1980 and 1994 there were almost 3000 international alliances formed between firms in the US, Japan, and Europe in information technology businesses and about 1300 in biotechnology during the same period. These two sectors have been the main focus for such alliances in recent years, with new materials research coming a distant third. The most common alliances are between US firms, followed by those between US and European companies.

While many people argue that MNCs help in the "technology transfer" between countries, the overall picture is very mixed. To the extent that an MNC has an "ownership advantage" in technological knowledge, it may be unwilling to share it with other firms, particularly those in foreign countries.

THE FINANCING OF MNCS

Since the 1970s, there has been a gradual deregulation of stock markets across the world and barriers to the free movement of capital have been dropping. This has had the effect of reducing the cost of capital for many firms, enabling them to invest more for growth and undertake more mergers and acquisitions.

Companies that are forced to finance their operations in an illiquid domestic market are likely to suffer from a limited availability of capital and, often, a higher cost of capital – many companies in smaller countries are in this position, as are small private firms everywhere who do not have easy access to stock and bond markets. Capital markets in many countries are "segmented," meaning that the required rate of return on stocks and bonds in that market are different from comparable rates in developed markets such as the US and London.

Causes of segmentation include regulatory controls, lack of "transparency" of information, insider trading, political risk, and cronyism – for example, during the Suharto regime in Indonesia which collapsed in 1997, firms that did not reward the Suharto family were unlikely to enjoy favorable treatment from local banks or regulators.

Since the 1980s, many companies have been able to escape the limitations of their home capital markets to access finance globally. This involves a much higher level of information disclosure, and the need for a continuous effort to maintain positive investor relations, both of which are very costly.

It is not necessarily easy for a company to raise equity globally for the first time. They must raise their profile to foreign investors and demonstrate a good track record. In general, investment bankers advise firms to begin the process by issuing bonds abroad first rather than equity.

American Depositary Receipts (ADRs) are certificates issued by international banks that represent underlying shares issued in a company's home market. Shares are held on deposit by the bank to guarantee the ADRs and are regulated by the US authorities; this often makes ADRs more attractive to investors, particularly in the US, than purchasing shares on the country's home stock exchange, which can be expensive and problematic for foreigners.

The goal for most companies is to issue shares on the London Stock Exchange, NASDAQ, or the New York Stock Exchange. These markets provide the most liquidity and greatest access to investors globally. The intense public scrutiny that comes with such a high profile listing means that firms need to have a good business story to tell – troubled firms from small countries are unlikely to find that global equity issues lead to a happy ending.

As with equity, the cost of borrowing abroad may be cheaper. Although debt may be easier to raise abroad than equity, international debt has special problems because of fluctuating exchange rates and interest rates. As with any borrowing, companies need to try to match the length of time of the loan to their capacity to repay. There is a very wide variety of debt instruments available globally, ranging from very short-term loans from banks to bonds with a maturity of many years. The cost and availability of these depend greatly on the credit rating of the firm itself and of its home country, but overall, most firms have far fewer constraints and a better range of choices when borrowing abroad than they do at home. Types of borrowing available include the following.

» International bank loans – lines of credit and syndicated loans (for large sums) offer flexibility and comparatively low interest rates.

» Euronotes and Euro-commercial paper – short to medium-term loans denominated in currencies that are held outside their own countries and are thus freer from the risk of government intervention.

» Eurobonds – these are medium to long-term debts that are traded between lenders and sold outside the country in whose currency the bond is denominated, giving flexibility and freedom from government regulation. Some of them are equity-related, meaning that they may be converted for shares on terms set by the borrower.

BEST PRACTICE: NOVO

In the late 1970s, Novo Industri, a Danish pharmaceutical company, recognized that its cost of capital was higher than its main foreign competitors and decided to try to escape the limitations of the Danish securities market to seek finance abroad. Furthermore, it was clear that the company would never be able to raise enough capital domestically to fund its promising growth opportunities. Large sums were needed to finance factories and research, and delays would mean that its foreign competitors would simply grab control of markets before Novo could enter them. Novo could not hope to fund its growth by reinvesting its profits because the process would be too slow and it would miss the opportunity to expand. The company had a good track record in its operations and excellent niche market strength worldwide.

At the time, Danish investors were not allowed to invest in foreign stocks and bonds in the private sector, so they tended to ignore developments in foreign securities markets and foreign stock analysts tended to ignore Denmark. Most Danish firms did not publish annual reports in English (although Novo did) and did not try to reconcile or translate their results into US or British accounting principles. High taxes on share profits had almost completely driven Danish private investors out of the stock market and price/earnings ratios of firms were low – Novo, like others, was trading at a P/E of 5. Danish stock prices tended to move up and down in tandem.

In 1978, Novo raised $20mn in convertible Eurobonds outside Denmark and obtained a listing on the London Stock Exchange. In the short term this actually increased the cost of capital when investors at home balked at the convertibility of the bonds, which had the potential of "diluting" the stock by increasing the number of shares in issue. Novo's share price dropped by nearly a third.

The following year, US investors became enthusiastic about the potential of biotechnology. In 1980 Novo promoted itself in New York and US investors began to buy its shares and convertible bonds in London. By the end of the year its share price was double its 1997 price and the company was 30% foreign-owned.

In 1981, Novo sought to expand its appeal to US investors by creating American Depositary Receipts (ADRs), obtaining an over-the-counter listing on NASDAQ and preparing for a listing on the New York Stock Exchange. The challenge was to prepare accounts according to US accounting standards and to fulfil the stringent information disclosure rules in the US. Its share price continued to rise, and the Danish investment community persistently described the company as grossly overvalued. When Novo made a $61mn share issue in New York, Danish investors sold hard, while US investors piled in, confident that the NYSE listing would provide adequate liquidity, which had previously been a worry. The company had achieved its objectives – access to much more capital at a significantly lower cost.

KEY LEARNING POINTS

- » Multinational companies and their affiliates are a hugely important element in world trade, accounting for around a third of the world's GDP. Although the biggest MNCs are concentrated in a few sectors, such as oil and autos, the diversity of MNC businesses is very wide. Since the 1980s, there has been a substantial growth in the number of MNCs from newly industrialized countries, particularly in East Asia, a region that has become a third major force in world trade (the others being the US and Europe).
- » MNCs can have substantial effects on the economies of countries and there is tension between them and governments who, while wanting the benefits that foreign MNCs can bring, wish to regulate their activities.
- » Companies have substantial opportunities to improve their financial position by issuing shares or borrowing in the global markets. While the biggest MNCs enjoy these benefits as a

matter of course, many smaller firms are hampered by regulations, high costs, and limited available capital at home. Although the "escape" to global financing is difficult and costly, many well-run firms have succeeded in achieving this during the last two decades.

- Although a listing on a major world stock market, such as the New York Stock Exchange, offers the potential for a large, liquid supply of capital, companies need to manage the process of getting there very carefully. Many firms begin by issuing Eurobonds, which helps to raise profile and gain credibility amongst international investors, and then graduate to listings on foreign exchanges.

NOTE

1 Krasner, S. (1996) Power, Politics, Institutions and Transnational Relations. In: *Bringing Transnational Relations Back In* (ed. T. Risse-Kappen) Cambridge University Press, Cambridge.

The State of the Art

This chapter looks at the most controversial issues in globalization. Movements against globalization are gathering momentum; what are the issues? The reality of the EU's policies and problems. How can the developing world be helped?

» The anti-globalization backlash: Seattle and beyond
» Krugman on GATT and the WTO
» The European Union: restructuring business
» Vodafone and Mannesmann – the deal that changed everything
» The European Union: enlargement
» EMU
» The EU and agriculture
» The developing world: food, development, growth, debt, and aid
» Misdirecting resources: Peruvian car manufacturing.

"[The state] is the great fictitious entity by which everyone seeks to live at the expense of everyone else."

Frédéric Bastiat, nineteenth century French economist

THE ANTI-GLOBALIZATION BACKLASH: SEATTLE AND BEYOND

In late 1999 a ministerial meeting of the World Trade Organization gathered in Seattle to outline the agenda for a new round of global trade talks (see Chapter 3 for an outline of the GATT agreements since WWII). It rapidly degenerated into a shambles as serious disagreements emerged, with the US, the EU, and developing countries crystallizing into warring camps. Outside, there were violent clashes between police and protesters, some of the 50,000 people, mainly trade unionists and environmentalists, who had converged on the city to demonstrate against trade-related issues. Eventually, the meeting collapsed.

During 2000 and 2001, an estimated one million people have taken part in demonstrations at meetings in Washington, Melbourne, Prague, Seoul, Nice, Barcelona, Washington DC, Quebec City, Gothenburg, and Genoa. At the time of writing, the WTO intends to make a second attempt to launch a new trade round in Doha, Qatar. For the first time in many years, the trend towards increased free trade and "globalization" looks under threat, with a world recession looming and well-organized political activism gaining strength.

Anne Krueger, deputy managing director of the IMF, said in 2001 that "the big risk is a slackening or slowdown in the rate of economic growth could lead to a sufficient downturn in economic activity to trigger a backlash among those who are now silent, but not necessarily supportive, of globalization." Anti-globalization is a form of protectionism that could reverse liberalization and "the long period of successful economic growth that the world has enjoyed." (See Fig. 6.1.)

The debate between protectionism and free trade has been raging for at least two centuries (see Chapter 8 for a discussion of the basic arguments) and although most economists are broadly in favor of free trade, many others – including many politicians – are not. The controversy is not merely a matter for theorists: a worldwide switch towards protectionism would have profound effects on industries and individual firms around the world.

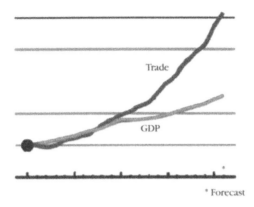

* Forecast

Fig. 6.1   World trade and GDP by volume, 1980–2000. (Source: WTO.)

While the anti-globalization movement has no unified agenda, it is a formidable collection of diverse groups, many of which are well-informed and in possession of substantial funds; for example, Anita Roddick, British CEO of the successful Body Shop eco-friendly cosmetics chain, was among the protesters at Seattle. The WTO, actually a modestly-funded body with only 530 employees that can only function by the consensus of its 142 member countries, has become a symbol of all that protesters see as wrong with the world – including the power of multinationals, ecological issues, Third World famine and debt, developed world job insecurity, and urban homogenization.

Defenders of the WTO point out that many of these issues are not confined to regions directly influenced by free trade, multinationals, or First World governments. For example, the ex-Soviet bloc has devastated much of its environment under its former command economies and the destruction of South-East Asian and Amazonian rain forests is driven largely by inward development (land grabbing). The noted economist Paul Krugman believes that in so far as global economic integration creates transparency it is probably a force for wiser environmental policies. He points out that states in the developed world are in any case hardly consistent in their pursuit of free trade policies, frequently finding reasons to block imports.

KRUGMAN ON GATT AND THE WTO

"To make agreements work there has to be some kind of quasi-judicial process that determines when ostensibly domestic measures are de facto a reimposition of trade barriers and hence a violation of treaty.

"Under the pre-WTO system, the General Agreement on Tariffs and Trade, this process was slow and cumbersome. It has now become swifter and more decisive ... The raw fact is that every successful example of economic development this past century – every case of a poor nation that worked its way up to a more or less decent, or at least dramatically better, standard of living – has taken place via globalization; that is, by producing for the world market rather than trying for self-sufficiency. Many of the workers who do that production for the global market are very badly paid by First World standards. But to claim that they have been impoverished by globalization, you have to carefully ignore comparisons across time and space – namely, you have to forget that those workers were even poorer before the new exporting jobs became available and ignore the fact that those who do not have access to the global market are far worse off than those who do."

The Uruguay trade round tabled a number of important issues to be resolved in the next round, notably the liberalization of trade in agriculture and services. Doing so would bring huge economic benefits – according to Drusilla Brown of Tufts University and Alan Deardorff and Robert Stern of the University of Michigan, a tariff reduction on agricultural and industrial products and services by 33% would increase world GDP by a one-off $600bn, more than eight times what was achieved by the Uruguay round.

Although easing the trade barriers to services will be comparatively easy, it will be much more difficult to obtain consensus on agriculture, which has always been one of the world's most protected industries in both rich and poor nations.

Countries with major agricultural exports, such as Australia and Argentina, have formed the "Cairns Group" to press for freer trade. While the US is officially committed to this, American protection and subsidy of domestic agriculture is very high, and it could be very difficult politically to achieve reform. Japan and the European Union (EU) are also hag-ridden by subsidy arrangements that protect their largely inefficient farming. The prospect of expanding the EU by admitting some Eastern European countries with vast, but vastly inefficient, farms is recognized as a looming policy problem.

The EU is pressing for the inclusion of three additional agenda items for the next trade round: competition, environment, and investment. Suspicions abound amongst other member states about the motives for broadening the agenda, particularly regarding the environment. While the EU says that it merely wants to clarify the WTO's rules on matters such as eco-labeling products and genetically modified foods, there are fears among the developing countries that the EU will use environmental issues as a pretext for blocking agricultural imports. The liberalization of food tariffs would transform the economies of many poorer countries.

The EU's politicians are under heavy pressure from their voters to keep food clean following the outbreak of mad cow disease and other scandals, and they point to the USA's resistance to agreement over global warming as evidence of a lack of American will for environmental reform.

Another problem is in agreeing anti-dumping rules. "Anti-dumping" is where a WTO country may impose high tariffs on items that it believes are being "dumped" (sold below cost) in its territory by another nation. Manufacturing nations such as Japan and South Korea are worried that anti-dumping rules can be misused to prevent imports of their goods to the US and Europe, while many poorer countries are starting anti-dumping investigations. China, which is the major target of anti-dumping tariffs after the US, is to participate in WTO for the first time, and negotiations are expected to be difficult.

Much is at stake here for the prosperity of individual businesses, nations and the world at large. For the first time in decades, the prospect of the economic pendulum swinging away from free trade towards protectionism is becoming a real possibility.

THE EUROPEAN UNION: RESTRUCTURING BUSINESS

The European Union (EU) is the largest trading bloc in the world, representing 40% of world trade and 20% of world GDP. Closer integration, economic reforms, and the potential enlargement of the Union to include parts of Eastern Europe present many opportunities and challenges for business.

A tradition of consensus and continuity has always been strong in much of northern continental Europe. The EU way of doing business has tended to be "caring" and stakeholder-orientated, in contrast to the "Anglo-Saxon" model of the US and, to a lesser extent, Britain. On the continent, employee protection, heavy regulation, oligopolies, and a large public sector have been an apparently permanent fact of life.

During the 1990s, Japan's go-go economy went into reverse. US firms restructured and surged ahead while large companies in continental Europe did poorly, failing, on average, to make enough profits to cover their cost of capital. By 1999, returns had improved to an average 14% on invested capital, but this was still much lower than the US figure of 27%. Today, everything is changing. Globalization, monetary union, deregulation, and privatization have stimulated firms to try to become more efficient.

VODAFONE AND MANNESMANN – THE DEAL THAT CHANGED EVERYTHING

Mannesmann, a giant German telephone company, had sought investment in the US and Britain during the 1990s to help fund its expansion in Europe, largely by friendly acquisition. To do so, it had to adopt the standards of accounting and information disclosure expected in the US and UK stock markets. By 1999, 60% of the company was in the hands of institutional investors in the US and UK.

Hostile takeovers were frowned upon in continental Europe. Legal barriers, trade unions, and consensual politics combined to prevent what were seen as an undesirable practice. In Germany, there had not been a single case of a hostile bid succeeding.

Vodafone AirTouch, a fast-growing British mobile telephone operator, achieved the unthinkable in 1999 when it successfully launched a hostile takeover of Mannesmann. A key factor was that the foreign investors in the German firm supported the bid – there was no controlling shareholding to block the sale, which set a record as the world's largest-ever hostile takeover.

The deal was widely perceived as a crucial event in the penetration of the "equity culture" into Europe. No European company could feel invulnerable to attack, and the wave of mergers and management buyouts, already underway, surged, driven largely by US investment.

The ownership of large continental firms has tended to be closely held among a small number of allies, in contrast to the British and American firms where there are generally very large numbers of shareholders. Until recently, the identity of owners could easily be kept secret on the continent, and control has been achieved by such techniques as issuing special categories of shares to insiders that have enormously enhanced voting rights – up to 1000 times that of ordinary shares in the case of Sweden. Using this method, Investor, a large Swedish holding company, owns 2.7% of Ericsson yet has 22% of the shareholders' votes.

Complex cross holdings between firms and banks are another way of retaining control. In 1999, according to a study by Marco Becht, of ECARES and Ailsa Röell, of Princeton University, over 50% of listed firms in Germany, Austria, Italy, and Belgium had more than half their voting rights in the hands of one shareholder or controlling group. Pressure from international investors is breaking up this ownership pattern.

The M&A boom may eventually wane, but other business reforms are also occurring. Competition for increasingly globalized markets are forcing large companies to restructure, while the advent of the single currency, the euro, offers opportunities for economies of scale within the EU, leveling prices and driving them downwards. Deregulation has radically reduced the price of telephone calls, while state-owned firms, such as German and Italian railways, are preparing for privatization. Inefficient companies are unlikely to survive for long.

THE EUROPEAN UNION: ENLARGEMENT

In the post-war ruins of continental Europe, industrialized countries were faced with the problem of how to rebuild their ravaged economies. In 1952, seven years after the end of WWII, France, West Germany, Italy, Belgium, Holland, and Luxembourg formed the European Coal and Steel Community (ECSC) to promote free trade between its members in what were then vital resources. It was hugely successful, and in 1958, following the 1957 Treaty of Rome, a far more ambitious project, the European Economic Community (EEC), now known as the European Union (EU), was formed with the intention of abolishing all barriers to the movement of goods, capital, and people between its member countries. This "customs union" is to be followed eventually by "economic union," entailing a complete harmonization of member states' economic policies.

In 1973, the six member group expanded to nine with the admission of Denmark, the UK, and Eire. Greece, Spain, and Portugal joined during the 1980s and Austria, Finland, and Sweden joined in 1995. The Maastricht Treaty, signed in 1992, is regarded as a major step towards closer political and economic union between EU members. Achieving further integration has not been an easy matter because member states are very diverse in terms of population size, unemployment levels, living standards, industrial structures, and so on. For instance, while the UK has the second largest population, it has the lowest proportion of agricultural workers, the third largest GDP but only the tenth largest GDP per capita and the slowest growth rate since 1960.

Following the collapse of the Soviet Bloc in 1989, the EU promised to welcome Eastern Europe into the union as a final end to the Cold War. Progress has been slow, however, because of practical problems of integration. The EU's motives for enlargement are not naïve – if the East had been abandoned to chaos, "the very idea of European integration would have undermined itself and eventually self-destructed," said Joschka Fischer, Germany's foreign minister in 2000.

In 1998 the EU finally launched the enlargement program which now comprises of 13 applicant countries:

» Bulgaria, Cyprus, Czech Republic;
» Estonia, Hungary, Latvia;
» Lithuania, Malta, Poland;
» Romania, Slovak Republic, Slovenia, and Turkey.

Restructuring these countries' systems to comply with EU requirements for democracy, the rule of law, economic stability, and the adoption of all current EU law is a hugely difficult task. At the time of writing the EU has postponed the first admissions to 2004 at the earliest.

The economic challenge is substantial. Admission of the 10 Central and Eastern European countries (Turkey is a separate case) would increase EU GDP by 5% but increase its population by 29%. The purchasing power of the average income would drop by 16%. While there are opportunities for growth, EU enlargement will be hard to digest.

EMU

Meanwhile, the introduction of the euro, the single currency, by most existing members is intended to complete the EU's single market by providing price transparency and removing forex risk. The strength of the euro will ultimately depend, as with all currencies, on how well the economy performs.

As we saw earlier, the euro has encouraged mergers and other deals. By creating a single market for capital it gives investors and firms more flexibility. For example, the number of corporate bonds being issued is increasing in Europe, mainly denominated in euros.

THE EU AND AGRICULTURE

One of the most problematic areas for the EU is its Common Agricultural Policy (CAP), run by the European Agricultural Guarantee and Guidance Fund (EAGGF), also known by its French title "Fonds Europeen d'Orientation et de Garantie Agricole" (FEOGA). When the

Treaty of Rome was signed in 1957 more than 20% of workers in the six original signatory countries were in agriculture, which was then very depressed. The CAP was created to revive the industry, protect it from imports, and provide stable incomes for its workers. Today the average proportion of agricultural workers in EU countries is 3.9%, a massive drop.

CAP guides farm production and guarantees incomes. Target prices are set for each product based on a profitable price for the highest-cost EU production area, rather than on world prices. The EU sets a guaranteed price at 7-10% below the target price, and intervenes to buy up produce if prices fall to this level. There are also separate target and guaranteed prices for individual products in many small areas within the EU. Guaranteeing prices to producers means that the EU must levy tariffs on competing imports. In addition, EU farm exporters receive subsidies to bring the export prices up to the guaranteed price.

Within a few years of the creation of the CAP, the output of small, high-cost farms predictably surged. The system of price intervention has created the well-known butter mountains, wine lakes, and so on, consisting of unwanted surpluses of produce ultimately paid for by EU consumers. Economists argue that CAP has resulted in resources being applied inefficiently within the EU and also that it discriminates against more efficient Third World producers that desperately need export income.

By the late 1980s, reforms to CAP resulted in limits being set on the production of certain products such as cereals, a reduction in guaranteed prices and effort to discourage highly intensive farming while protecting farm jobs and marginal farmers. Land has been taken out of use, with farmers being compensated for what is not produced. Arguments for further reform include the need to help the EU's 18.5 million unemployed (compared with the 7 million subsidized farmers) and the financial impossibility of subsidizing farmers at current rates in the potential new member states in Eastern Europe.

THE DEVELOPING WORLD: FOOD, DEVELOPMENT, GROWTH, DEBT, AND AID

Conceivably, the developed world could ignore the plight of poorer nations, turn inwards and still prosper. Many policy-makers believe, however, that helping poorer countries to help themselves is not a matter of charity, but rather one of enlightened self-interest. The president of the World Bank, James D. Wolfenson, stated this view clearly in a 1997 speech, saying:

> "We can insulate ourselves from whole sections of the world for which crisis is real and daily but which to the rest of us is largely invisible. But we must recognize that we are living with a time bomb and unless we take action now, it could explode in our children's faces."

> "If we do not act, in thirty years the inequities will be greater. With population growing at 80 million a year, instead of 3 billion living on under $2 a day, it could be as high as 5 billion . . . in thirty years, the number of conflicts may be higher. Already we live in a world which last year alone saw twenty six interstate wars and 23 million refugees . . . without economic hope we will not have peace. . ."

> And economics is fundamentally changing the relationships between the rich and the poor nations. Over the next twenty five years, growth in China, India, Indonesia, Brazil and Russia will likely redraw the economic map of the world as the share in global output of the developing and transition economies doubles. Today these countries represent 50% of the world's population but only 8% of its GDP. Their share in world trade is a quarter of that of the European Union. By the year 2020, their share in world trade could be 50% more than Europe's . . . we share the same challenge. The fight against poverty is the fight for peace, security and growth for us all."

> *James D Wolfenson*[1]

In short, many feel that the developed world cannot afford to turn its back on the rest of the world if it is to assure its own future prosperity in the long term – the risks are simply too high. There is a broad agreement among interests as diverse as big business, government, and the anti-WTO groups that reducing the world's gross inequalities is a vital long-term objective.

The devil is in the detail. While some countries have had notable development success over many decades, such as Japan, Singapore, and South Korea, many nations suffer from intractable problems that economic theory has difficulty in either explaining or curing. The key issues are inter-related.

» Food – it is generally recognized that human activity is the principal cause of the endemic malnutrition and periodic famines that devastate parts of the developing world. Poor farming methods, a lack of environmental controls, bad transport infrastructure, a failure to stockpile food, and military action to cut food supplies have been significant features of the famines in countries such as Biafra, Ethiopia, Somalia, and Rwanda.

» As we have seen, the developed world does not allow a free market in its own agriculture, with a tendency to keep prices high and encourage surpluses through subsidy. Many LDCs have taken the opposite approach: keeping food prices artificially low for the benefit of their politically-active urban populations. The problem is that farmers reduce their output and switch to other crops. For example, Mexico used to keep domestic corn prices low to maintain a cheap price for tortillas, the staple food of city dwellers. Farmers switched to crops free of price controls and corn shortages increased to the point that it had to be imported.

» Developed world farming is highly productive overall: one US farmer can produce enough to feed 80 people. In contrast, most LDC farmers can barely feed their own immediate families. Low agricultural productivity in LDCs may often be due to the extreme difficulty that farmers face in introducing new cultivation methods. Better seeds, machinery, fertilizers, and irrigation systems are expensive and without a stable system of agricultural bank lending, a poor farmer may well be making a rational choice when he decides to ignore new technologies rather than take on a very risky debt burden. An urgent need for land reform is also a factor in some regions, particularly in Latin America where 2% of landowners possess 75% of the farmland. In China, for instance, allowing farmers to own their own land and sell their produce has had a dramatically increased output.

» Development strategies – until the 1970s the majority of LDCs and their advisers believed that the key to economic development was to industrialize. Trying to mimic the structures of developed economies, however, is increasingly seen as ineffective and in recent years more emphasis has been placed on agriculture. Large agricultural projects such as dams and irrigation systems require heavy investment, but many others, such as farming education programs, do not require large sums of money. Striking a balance between agricultural and industrial development is now seen as the best development path. "Import substitution," where an LDC sets up industries to produce goods that replace imported products, is widely believed to have been a failure. By protecting local fledging industries with high tariffs, gross economic inefficiencies were created.

MISDIRECTING RESOURCES: PERUVIAN CAR MANUFACTURING

Peru has a population of 24 million, most of whom cannot afford to buy a car. In the 1970s the country had six different car manufacturers, all with low output. These firms were unable to benefit from economies of scale (see Chapter 7, Ford) and their cost of production was much higher than world market prices, making exports impossible. Valuable resources were spent on auto production that could have been better employed elsewhere.

» Promoting exports has been a more successful approach than import substitution. Japan's dramatic postwar success in developing into the world's second largest economy was based largely on exporting manufactured goods. Other East Asian economies, such as Singapore, Taiwan, and Korea, have also had success in this approach.
» "Structural adjustment" is the effort to reduce the size of the public sector in LDCs, control inflation, encourage private saving and investment through tax reform, and reduce national debt. These are all pro-free market measures that have been strongly promoted by the IMF and the World Bank during the 1980s and 1990s in response to the problem that while many LDCs' GDP per head grew in the 60s and 70s, much of the population did not share in the new wealth.
» Population growth – in the 1800s Thomas Malthus, an English economist, predicted that the population of Europe and America would grow faster than the food supply, leading to disastrous poverty.

He did not foresee the improvements in agricultural methods that transformed productivity, nor that Western population growth would begin to slow. But are the LDCs living in a Malthusian world? LDC populations are growing at about 1.7% annually, compared with 0.5% in industrial nations, which means that at the present rate LDC populations will double every 41 years. Looking at the parlous state of many LDC economies, it is daunting to contemplate such a massive increase in their populations.

» Figure 2.1 in Chapter 2 shows that since the Industrial Revolution the world's population has grown dramatically. Not much is known about the possible consequences, but the fear is that LDCs will not be able to support massive increases in the number of children. One interesting approach to analyzing fertility patterns is to look at why parents choose to have large or small families. Recent studies suggest that parents in the developing world may be acting rationally when they choose to have large families because children supply valuable labor and are the only way to ensure financial support in old age. If incomes rise or there are increased employment opportunities for women, the opportunity cost of having a child increases (there are better things to do) and birth rates may start to fall. Economic development, therefore, may be the answer to reducing the rate of population growth.

KEY LEARNING POINTS

» In 1999 a backlash against globalization began that has swept around the world, focusing on the WTO as its chief target. In 2001 a senior WTO official remarked that the major problem with WTO/GATT is not that countries are against free trade, but that its implications have not been properly explained to the public.

» The US, the EU, and the developing world have contending objectives for the next trade round, with the developing world wanting a stronger voice in negotiations. China is to join the WTO for the first time as part of its continuing efforts to open up to international business.

» During the 1990s, the tide turned in continental Europe as corporations began to try to become more efficient. Pressure from foreign investors is encouraging better disclosure, broader ownership, and a wave of deal-making. Global competition and the single European market are forcing companies to use their capital more effectively and expand outside their national borders.

» Plans for EU enlargement to admit 13 new member countries are being delayed as applicants need to converge economically and politically with EU norms before they join. The new members are poor – enlargement is being handled delicately to avoid problems.

» The EU's single currency has boosted investment and company restructuring for efficiency by providing a single European market for investment capital. It is expected to help lower prices by removing exchange rate risk within the EU and creating price transparency.

» The EU's agriculture is inefficient because of the protectionist Common Agricultural Policy (CAP) that favors farmers over consumers. Created at a time when 20% of EU workers were in agriculture (there are now less than 4%), the CAP is being reformed. Further reform will be needed to cope with the admission of Eastern European countries that have large agricultural sectors.

» There is a consensus that the rich countries cannot afford *not* to help poorer countries develop. While the NICs have successfully transformed themselves into vigorous free market economies, other LDCs are in serious trouble. The current emphasis is on encouraging free markets, a balanced mix of better agriculture and industry, and exporting rather than import substitution. It is hoped that the rapid population growth in LDCs will self-adjust downwards as nations get richer – as it has, for instance, in Japan and Singapore.

NOTE

1 "The Challenge of Inclusion," address to World Bank Board of Governors, Hong Kong, September 23, 1997.

In Practice: Global Success Stories

Specific challenges facing three very different MNCs and how they are responding.

- » Ford Motor Company – life as a giant
- » NTT DoCoMo – the battle for new global markets
- » Nestlé – global corporate responsibility.

"If I was to describe to you a business where you have to manage worldwide overcapacity, huge fixed costs, government-supported industry in certain countries and too many players, you would have to be mad to say it's something you want to get into."

Bill Ford, chairman of Ford Motor Company

FORD MOTOR COMPANY – LIFE AS A GIANT

Ford Motor Company is the quintessential multinational. Henry Ford, the firm's founder, was a key figure in the development of mass-production methods that had such a transforming effect on economic growth in the twentieth century – in 1913, he achieved a 90% reduction in car assembly time, a classic illustration of how economic growth can be achieved by finding ways of producing more using existing resources.

The world's second largest car manufacturer after General Motors, in 2000 Ford had a turnover of $170bn but a relatively low income before taxes of $8.2bn. The company employs nearly 350,000 people across the world and sold some 7.4 million cars and trucks in 2000.

Like its main competitors, its principal markets are in the developed countries of North America and Western Europe – although Ford has a controlling share of Mazda, it only sells some 26,000 units in Japan, approximately half of its sales in Argentina.

The problem: overcapacity

A new car is a "big ticket" item for the consumer, costing a substantial proportion of annual salary, if not more, which means that people often have to borrow money to make their purchase. To persuade more customers to buy cars, Ford and its rivals have developed substantial consumer loan and corporate leasing operations. In Ford's case, its "Financial Services Sector" generated $28.8bn in revenues in 2000.

For many decades, car manufacturers operated a "push" system, producing vehicles in huge numbers in expensive plants and delivering them to the consumer via a tightly controlled network of dealers. As more and more manufacturers around the world entered the field, the markets of the developed world progressed towards near-saturation despite valiant efforts to introduce new product types in the hope of extending markets.

Today, says Jacques Nasser, Ford's CEO, "If you look at it in a macro sense, there's too much capacity... If you're not fit and lean, and are burdened with excess assets that are not utilized well, it's not fair to the customers and employees and shareholders." This is something of an understatement – auto pundits argue that worldwide there is an overcapacity of some 30%, severely destabilizing the market, deflating prices, reducing profits that are already low, and encouraging governments to adopt protectionist policies to preserve jobs.

In the long term, however, there are plenty of potential car buyers in the developing world, particularly in China, South-East Asia, Eastern Europe, and Latin America. With trade barriers falling, the established car companies are increasing their presence in these regions. One difficulty is that most of these potential consumers cannot afford to purchase vehicles at present – future sales will depend on overall economic growth. Another problem is that developing countries may not have an infrastructure that is adequate to support modern automotive plants that need high quality machine and engineering support groups associated with other industries. Thirdly, there is a need for a workforce with the skills and training necessary to manufacture and assemble components and subsystems, and to manage and maintain the equipment. Finally, a country has to have a logistical system able to move supplies and components in sufficient quantities and to deliver the completed product efficiently.

Getting even bigger: economies of scale

Car manufacturing is a mature industry, with vast firms dominating the markets, particularly through their ability to achieve economies of scale. As with other firms, Ford is over-dependent on the North American market and finds its numerous plants across the world difficult to manage because of restrictive labor agreements. The advent of e-commerce and pressure from the environmental lobby also represent major challenges to profit growth – laws regulating exhaust emissions and fuel consumption are increasing in severity.

Analysts expect only the biggest firms to survive in the medium term. Ford is one of only six "first tier" companies worldwide that are likely to dominate the market in years to come. Ford and its rivals in the "Global Six" have three main strategies they can adopt.

1 *Reducing the asset base to free capital for more focused investment.* In 1998, Ford gathered all of its component divisions into a single entity and created Visteon as a global supplier, retaining the core businesses of engine, chassis, and assembly. Visteon was then "spun off" as a separate public company in 2000 by distributing its shares tax-free as a dividend to existing Ford shareholders; one effect of this was to reduce the number of employees by some 7%. General Motors also adopted this strategy by divesting Delphi.

2 *Acquire other firms and build alliances.* This is again principally an effort to cut costs while gaining control of more product brands. There has been a frenzy of industry mergers in the last few years, with Ford purchasing Land Rover for $2.6bn in 2000, Volvo's car business in 1999 for $6.45bn and Kwik-Fit, a European light repair chain, in 1999 for approximately $1.4bn. With the advent of e-commerce threatening to shorten the supply chain, Ford has entered into a purchasing joint venture, Covisint, with GM, DaimlerChrysler, Renault and Nissan, intended to create a business-to-business supplier exchange on a single global Internet portal. This move could reduce manufacturing costs by up to $3000 per vehicle. Covisint hopes to become the world's largest virtual marketplace, moving all auto commodity purchases onto the net. If it is successful, more e-alliances are to come in distribution, retailing, and vehicle marketing.

3 *Making superior products.* Customer loyalty is particularly valuable in the auto industry, where it is estimated that the cost of marketing a product to an existing customer is about 20% of attracting a new one. A "superior" product can be defined in many ways, but it essentially revolves around customer perception which varies internationally. US consumers want convenience, Europeans need fuel economy and the Japanese require compact vehicles, for instance.

R&D – from basic research in materials and methods to vehicle design – is vital. By distributing the R&D role globally, there is an opportunity to take advantage of local pockets of expertise for all vehicle programs, and to "localize" designs based on global platform standards and common components for the local consumer. The R&D challenge is to find ways of fulfilling these needs while pushing the standardization of parts and design to reduce costs. Ford has relocated product development centers to the countries where specific products are sold to help deal with national preferences. In 2000, it introduced the "Think" line of electric-powered vehicles with plastic bodies based on technology purchased in Norway. Said CEO Jacques Nasser, "we really believe that consumers want alternative products . . . We're using the Think as a way of incubating and hatching new technologies such as fuel cells. The technology will then migrate to other vehicles." Ford has also announced plans to sell a hybrid gas-electric sedan using an internal combustion engine mated to an electric motor and achieving a fuel economy of 80 miles to the gallon – and has suggested that the US government create a tax credit for such vehicles to offset their increased purchase cost.

As a prime mover in one of the twentieth century's chief engines of growth Ford has always been involved with governments. Prior to the development of fascism in the 1930s, Ford had little regulatory difficulty in entering foreign markets, but by 1939 it had been driven out of Japan and much of Europe. Despite its global reach today, the company is an example of just how little large MNCs can be truly said to be globalized: about 66% of units are sold in North America and most of the rest in Europe, with unit sales in the rest of the world accounting for less than 10% of the total. It undoubtedly remains a family-controlled company with a culture based firmly on its national origins. For example, Ford first purchased stock in Mazda in 1979 in the hope of acquiring Japanese skills and expertise, but the two companies did not exchange anything other than finished vehicles. It was only when Ford acquired a controlling position in 1996 that true synergies and collaboration began to emerge – the first jointly designed vehicle for the US market is the Ford Escape/Mazda Tribute.

Ford's business is highly vulnerable to state regulation, which varies considerably from country to country. As well as the problems of trade barriers and the ever-present pressures to protect the workforce from downsizing, laws on safety standards and governing fuel economy and emissions have dramatic effects on vehicle costs and designs. Attempts to design and integrate components separately for each country's set of regulations led to massive inefficiencies and waste, as components built for one market could not be used in others, leading to local oversupply and shortages because of minor regulatory changes. To solve this, Ford has developed a sophisticated strategy of "homologation" in its engineering process to address these problems. All components are evaluated against all relevant regulations globally to ensure that components from one region can be used in any other on the same platform as often as possible. The impact of this and other standardization procedures for fasteners and connectors alone frees significant amounts of capital for the company to use in more productive ways.

One of the problems of introducing environmentally-friendly vehicles is that they are more expensive for the consumer, at least until a mass market can be created. As was mentioned earlier, Ford suggested that its electric/internal combustion engine hybrid should attract a tax credit to offset its higher retail price. In effect it is arguing that governments should help to pay for creating a world of environmentally sound vehicles. Lobbying of this kind is generally done through trade associations such as the AAMA in the US, ASAA in Europe, and Working Party 29, a world forum for harmonizing regulations through the United Nations.

"It is tough because governments guard their prerogative to set standards. Outside groups have also been suspicious that we're trying to lower standards when we're really not. We're just trying to harmonize them, saying you choose the right thing. Certainly let's do the research jointly, so that we all can say, 'here are the results,' and we agree on that. But there has been some opposition. . . we've made some progress, in terms of trying to get some simple standards harmonized between Europe and the US," says Martin Zimmerman, Executive Director, Government Relations and Corporate Economics at Ford.

KEY INSIGHTS

- Technical change often leads to increased worker productivity and lower costs, leading to increased output and economic growth without adding new resources. Henry Ford's creation of mass production techniques in the early twentieth century is a well-known example of this.

» To some extent Ford is a victim of its own extraordinary success. Car manufacturing has developed from a cottage industry to maturity over the last century, and the major markets of the developed world have little room for growth.

» Although millions in the developing world would like to purchase a car, they do not have the means to do so. In Brazil, for instance, only 1 in 11 people owns a car. The need for a good infrastructure, high-tech suppliers and skilled labor are other major barriers to market growth in the short to medium term.

» Cost cutting has become paramount. Rather than integrating vertically, Ford and others have aggressively pursued mergers and alliances during the 1990s. In a heavily regulated environment where the weakest firms will not remain independent for long, Ford has chosen to concentrate on its core business – making cars – and divested its parts division, Visteon. In an attempt to eliminate duplication and cut costs, transnational auto manufacturers like Ford are changing their relationships with their parts suppliers, reducing their number, attempting to collaborate more closely on product design and development and outsourcing many processes.

» Ford may be a global company, but its strengths derive from its US roots. Transnationalism brings huge headaches in the regulatory sphere, with every national market subject to different, constantly changing rules. Ford's "homologation" design system attempts to minimize the costs of conforming to a multitude of standards across the globe.

NTT DOCOMO – THE BATTLE FOR NEW GLOBAL MARKETS

For decades the telecommunications industry was regarded as an uneventful collection of state-controlled utilities. Deregulation and the advent of the Internet and mobile telephony changed everything – today it is a "hot" sector with huge sums being risked by a large number of private competitors worldwide. Mobile telephony was one of the great successes of the 1990s. By the end of the decade, the number of mobile subscribers worldwide was over 400 million; in OECD countries, about 1 in 4 people had mobile phones, whereas 10 years before the figure was about 1 in 100, an average annual growth for the decade of 56%. In 1999, global mobile revenues were around $300bn.

There is no sign of a slowdown. Global revenues are expected to double to $600bn by 2003 and the number of subscribers may reach 1.2 billion by 2004. As might be expected, the three largest regions in the cellular market are the richest areas – Western Europe, North America, and Asia-Pacific – but consumers in poorer countries are "leapfrogging" to mobile phones, especially where fixed line telephones are hard to obtain or expensive. Much of the growth is being by the introduction of prepaid tariffs that attract lower-income groups such as the young or people in LDCs. Market saturation is not expected in developed countries until 2010.

Free marketeers applaud these developments that have transformed an industry dominated by state-owned monopolies. The OECD, for instance, argues that, "Analysis clearly shows a strong correlation between market growth and market openness. During the 1990s, those markets that had liberalized the most, and had four or more operators, have consistently outperformed markets with monopolies, duopolies, or three operators."

The extremely rapid growth of mobile telephony has thrown companies and regulators into chaos, however. There are a number of reasons for this, including the following.

» Mobile use is outpacing fixed line use in some areas, threatening revenues from the traditional phone business.
» The appetite for data transmission grows and grows – huge investments are needed in infrastructure that can accommodate the increase in traffic. The appetite for speed just grows and grows.
» No one is quite sure how to price services or licenses in a rapidly changing market.
» Manufacturers are competing fiercely to introduce newer, "smarter" products, in many cases before there is the infrastructure or compelling content to make them appealing to consumers.

» There is also fierce competition between a multitude of rival technological standards, confusing and frustrating consumers.
» The convergence of e-commerce, the Internet, and mobile telephony
is a huge headache for companies in the industry – they all want to
be in the game, but it is not clear which strategies and services will
ultimately be successful.

Telcos have borrowed massively to fund their growth, and by 2001
many of them were in trouble. In Europe, telecom firms paid $115bn
for government licenses to operate "3G" services, the new (third)
generation mobile technology. Stock prices collapsed as technical bugs
slowed the introduction of 3G. British Telecom, Deutsche Telekom,
Vodafone, and others began to ask European governments for some of
their money back. So far, governments have not accommodated them
and the debt-heavy telcos are now potential acquisition targets.

Japan's largest telco, the Nippon Telegraph and Telephone Corporation (NTT DoCoMo) is in a position to take advantage of the situation as
it obtained free 3G licenses in Japan. Among the $15.5bn in recent NTT
acquisitions are a 16% stake in AT&T and investments in KPN Mobile of
the Netherlands, the UK's Hutchison 3G, Hong Kong-based Hutchison
Telephone, and Taiwan. To help finance this, DoCoMo carried out
Japan's biggest sale of new shares by a listed company in January 2001.
In 2001 the company also took out a $10bn loan from five Japanese
banks and sold $180bn worth of 5- and 10-year bonds. An additional
¥100bn in bonds were issued in October, 2001.

I-mode, its proprietary mobile service offering Internet access, has
been a huge hit in Japan, capturing 22 million subscribers by mid-2001.
Although NTT has also launched the world's first 3G service, it believes
that it will not be the key to future revenue growth in the short to
medium term. I-mode's boss, Kei-ichi Enoki, commented in 2001 that,
"I don't think the business model will fundamentally change from 2G
to 3G. The essence of the cellular phone business will be the same."
DoCoMo feels that 3G technology will not be able to carry the large
video and sound clips that many see as a potentially hugely lucrative
new service because costs to the user will be prohibitive.

While the jury is still out on 3G and its successor 4G, NTT has been
making hay in the meantime with i-mode. The company purchased
a large stake in AOL Japan to provide its mobile service with more

net-related facilities and content. I-mode users can currently access tens of thousands of Web sites offering news, information, banking services, shopping, ticketing and reservations, sports, dating, character and melody download, and, importantly, access to the outside Web at large (although sites must be suitably formatted for the small screen).

Like its Japanese rivals KDDI and J-phone, DoCoMo has solved the problem of how to charge customers for content. I-mode mobile Internet surfers are charged small monthly fees to access certain ''official'' sites with a few clicks, while users must input the URL addresses of ''unofficial'' sites manually.

I-mode is an interesting solution to the problem mobile operators face in getting to the super-fast, seamlessly integrated mobile Internet that everybody wants. With minor modifications of established technology, such as HTML (the Web page design language) and fees based on packets of data downloaded (giving the user unlimited connection time), i-mode offers users a far more attractive and convenient service than the US and European attempts at introducing Wireless Application Protocol (WAP). I-mode is, in effect, more of a brand of innovative services than a ground-breaking technology.

NTT sees its DoCoMo subsidiary as being more than a mobile operator: ''Our information distribution services businesses now stand on the verge of significant growth. As mobile multimedia develops, DoCoMo intends to support not only 'person-to-person' communications but also 'person-to-machine' and 'machine-to-machine' communications. I-mode was a first step in this direction, linking people and computers. At once, mobile phones were transformed from communication tools into terminals for receiving information on a real-time basis. Examples of 'machine-to-machine' services include a system that monitors quantity and type of products remaining in vending machines and a service that allows remote control of machinery by a computer. Looking further ahead, anything that moves, including motor vehicles, is a candidate for wireless services. Looking at the potential for growth, the business possibilities are breathtaking.''

With the 2G-based i-Mode launch in 1998–99, DoCoMo had already shifted its view of the mobile phone business, deciding that data rather than voice was the way to add value. DoCoMo has stepped back from the fierce competition to win new mobile customers and is concentrating on extracting more revenue from its existing subscribers.

I-mode is not the "killer app" that will clinch the titanic battle for control of the world's mobile markets; time will tell, but it is more probable that it will ultimately be seen as an effective medium-term tactic to stay in a game which could be fought intensely for a decade or more and is as likely to be as powerful an agent for change as the Internet.

KEY INSIGHTS

» The ease and fluidity with which NTT has been able to acquire positions in, and alliances with, foreign telcos (as have foreign telcos in Japan with NTT's competitors) is indicative of just how much has been achieved by the process of globalization, in the sense of freer trade, technology exchange, and capital flows between the major trading blocs. In the 1970s, for instance, such deals would have been unthinkable.

» Nevertheless, there is little evidence here of the development of truly "transnational" MNCs. NTT has enjoyed favorable treatment over licenses in its mother country, Japan, while telcos of European origin fell foul of their own states' licensing policies. National origin continues to be a major factor in the intricate chess game played between MNCs and governments.

» The extraordinary speed of developments in communications has plainly outpaced governments' capacity to respond effectively. At the time of writing, a world recession looks likely, which may dampen down the exuberance of IT-based industries and give states a chance to catch up and consider just how much laissez-faire they are prepared to accept in what has been dubbed the "Information Age."

NESTLÉ – GLOBAL CORPORATE RESPONSIBILITY

Nestlé, the world's largest food company, was founded in 1867 by a Swiss pharmacist, Henri Nestlé, who developed the first substitute for breast milk for babies. Faced with a small domestic market, the company went global early. Today it has a total workforce of approximately

225,000 people in 479 factories scattered across 81 countries, with less than 2% of total sales being generated in Switzerland. Being a Swiss company, however, insulates Nestlé from some of the short-term pressures from financial markets – because quarterly reports are not required, the company is not affected by the four monthly share-price jitters that can disturb its major competitors in the US, and can concentrate on longer-term growth. That approach has paid off, producing an average annual increase in shareholder return of 20% over the last 10 years. The company's shares are listed on the stock exchanges of Zurich, London, Paris, and Frankfurt, with ADRs offered in the US by Morgan Guaranty.

Nestlé products are available in nearly every country around the world. It is the brand manager's dream, with more than 130 main brands in food and personal care products. 70% of the company's sales come from six worldwide corporate brands, Nestlé, Nescafé, Nestea, Maggi, Buitoni, and Friskies. For decades it has steadily acquired more well-known brands, including Findus frozen foods, Vittel mineral water, Crosse & Blackwell preserves and Rowntree confectionery. Its total sales were over $49bn in 2000, with profits of $3.7bn. About a third of sales are generated in the Americas and another third in Europe. The remainder is split roughly equally between food sales in the rest of the world and the global sales of pharmaceuticals and bottled water, which is managed as a separate division.

The company places great emphasis on expanding its markets geographically. "One of our major challenges and opportunities is to understand local consumer habits in the local environment. A classic reason for failure is to believe that a sound concept and a good product in one part of the world is enough in itself to ensure success in another part of the world. Understanding the local environment would probably imply adjustments to a product and to a concept ... There are some experiences that show the contrary, but in the food area, local understanding is fundamental," says Claudio Bartolini, senior vice president of Nestlé's Dairy Strategic Business Unit.

Nestlé has attracted criticism for its activities in LDCs over issues such as environmental practices, employment conditions, and its marketing methods. The best known controversy is over the company's original product, milk for babies. For 20 years pressure groups have promoted a boycott of the company's products on the grounds that powdered baby milk can cause unnecessary health problems when misused.

Like so many nineteenth century innovations, baby milk powder was a genuine advance. In the days before refrigeration, perishable food such as milk was hard to store, and any process that increased shelf-life was a boon. It was not until the 1960s that an awareness began to emerge of some of the problems of the overuse of processed foods – specifically, that they are not perfect nutritional substitutes for the unprocessed foods they replace. In the case of baby milk powder, the main objections center on medical arguments that breast feeding is preferable and the obvious need to follow the instructions for preparation. In developed countries this causes few problems, as mothers generally have good access to healthcare advice, are adequately nourished, and are sophisticated consumers.

In LDCs, however, circumstances are different. In the late 1970s, consumer groups began to claim that breastfeeding was declining in LDCs as mothers switched to substitutes, leading to higher infant mortality – estimates run as high as one million deaths annually. The health problems, they said, were due to several factors:

» no access to clean water to mix with the processed milk;
» lack of fuel leading to a failure to heat the milk to the correct temperature;
» mothers possibly being unable to read the instructions for preparation, and mixing the formula in the wrong proportions;
» mothers possibly overdiluting the formula in an effort to save money;
» a failure to sterilize bottles;
» the fact that, unlike breast milk, substitutes do not contain antibodies that protect infants from disease.

Consumer groups claimed that companies selling breast milk substitutes were exacerbating these problems by giving away large quantities of their products as part of their marketing strategy to promote brand loyalty. Nestlé, as the largest firm in the industry, was a major focus of their ire (its rivals in the baby milk business include Hipp, Milupa, and Meiji).

In 1979 a UNICEF/WHO-sponsored conference concluded that there was a need for a code of practice to govern the marketing of breast milk substitutes. The World Health Assembly, the official governing body of WHO, produced a code which Nestlé signed in 1984, restricting advertising, requiring labeling information on the hazards of use, and prohibiting companies from giving free samples, promoting the products in hospitals and clinics or employing nurses to advise mothers. The consumer groups agreed to suspend the boycott of Nestlé products that began in 1977.

Today, Nestlé endorses the code of practice, and states that it "does encourage and support exclusive breastfeeding as the best choice for babies during the first months of life" and "does warn mothers of the consequences of incorrect or inappropriate use of infant formula". It also says that it believes that "there is a legitimate market for infant formula when a safe alternative to breast milk is needed."

The code itself is not enforceable. In the 1980s and 1990s various countries, including the Philippines, Thailand, Kenya, Malaysia, Costa Rica, and Brazil, introduced controls over the marketing of baby milk. Consumer groups revived the boycott, claiming that Nestlé, along with industry competitors, were violating the spirit of the code, in particular by making donations of baby formula to hospitals. Ironically, increasing HIV infection in Africa has created a new demand for baby formula to prevent the spread of the disease, and there is now a dilemma for both companies and regulators over how to respond.

KEY INSIGHTS

» Firms with small home markets have to seek growth abroad. Like Nokia, the mobile phone maker (featured in Chapter 7 of the ExpressExec book Valuation), Nestlé took this leap in the late 1800s, merging with the Anglo-Swiss Condensed Milk Company, controlled by American Charles Page in 1878. With its broad diversity of products and decentralized management system, the company is one of the very few MNCs that could be described as "transnational." It is market-focused, concentrating on horizontal expansion, both geographically and by acquiring new products.

» Regional management of operations has enabled Nestlé to take advantage of local cultural biases and preferences to enhance the appeal of its products locally. Brands not known in Europe or North America are mainstays in Asia, like Milo, a milk-based chocolate drink. In many cases Nestlé markets identical products under different names in different regions.

» Most large companies, particularly those selling to consumers, are subject to intense public scrutiny by pressure groups, particularly in the developed world but increasingly also in LDCs. The days when such groups could be dismissed as radical extremists are long gone. Public attitudes have changed on many issues over the last few decades. Problems of LDC development, globalization, energy conservation, environmentalism, "green" and genetically-modified food, product labeling, and so on are everyday topics of discussion in the media and are important factors in government policy-making. They have profound effects on the way large companies do business. Like other firms, Nestlé has to respond to these issues, and actively participates in the process, publishing detailed information on its efforts at environmental conservation and adhering to a wide range of international codes of business practice.

» Nestlé has occasionally been accused of "going slow" on reform. It is hard to see how any large corporation could do otherwise. The challenge is how to continue to grow in a highly competitive business while acceding to the newer ideas on sustainable LDC development. Like Ford, Nestlé faces widely differing consumer demands and regulatory requirements across the world, and any change to packaging, product contents, or marketing strategy requires considerable expenditure of resources.

» The company's sales of breast milk substitutes in LDCs is said to have declined, although the precise details are not known. In a 1988 interview, a company spokesman was reported as saying "infant formula in developing countries is now less than 1 percent of our consolidated sales. It would be very easy simply to drop this matter, be rid of the controversy. Why don't we do it? Because we believe we fulfill a need."

Key Concepts and Thinkers

A more detailed look at some essential concepts that are not widely understood: the nature of the antagonism between protectionism and free trade; Keynes' contribution to managing the world's economy and more recent approaches; Alan Greenspan's role in the US economy; how productivity growth seems to be declining in the developed world – but it is hard to measure and involves many trade-offs; growth in the future – Paul Romer's view.

- » Glossary
- » Protectionism versus free trade
- » John Maynard Keynes (1883–1946)
- » Monetarism and Milton Friedman
- » Supply-side economics
- » Alan Greenspan
- » The productivity problem and growth
- » Paul Romer: new growth theory.

"An 'acceptable' level of unemployment means that the government economist to whom it is acceptable still has a job."

Anonymous

GLOSSARY

Aggregate demand – The total demand for goods and services in an economy.

Aggregate income – The total income of all production factors in a given period. It is exactly equal to aggregate output.

Aggregate output – The total amount of goods and services produced or supplied in a given period.

Balance of trade – The difference between a country's exports and imports.

Balance of payments – The accounting record of a country's transactions with the rest of the world in goods, assets, and services; also, the accounting record of its supply and demand for foreign currencies.

Capital flight – The escape of financial and human capital from countries offering low rates of return.

Command economy – An economy where central government sets prices, wages, and production targets.

Comparative advantage – There is much misunderstanding of this key concept. It is the idea that everyone benefits if each country specializes in producing the goods that it can generate most efficiently, relative to other countries, and imports those goods that other countries produce most efficiently. The USA produces some food crops more efficiently than China, while China produces clothing more efficiently. By selling these goods to one another, they both gain. See Chapter 2.

Depression – A severe and long-lasting recession (see "recession"). There is no consensus on precisely when a recession becomes a depression.

Federal Reserve System (the Fed) – The central bank in the US that monitors and influences the US money supply and interest rates.

GATT – An international agreement on trade first signed in 1947.

Great Depression – A period of severe unemployment and economic contraction during the 1930s.

Gross Domestic Product (GDP) – The total market value in a country of all final goods and services produced by units located there. Nominal GDP is the figure in today's money, while real GDP is the inflation-adjusted figure.

Gross National Product (GNP) – The total market value in a country of all final goods and services produced anywhere by units owned by that county's nationals.

Inflation – A general increase in prices.

International Monetary Fund (IMF) – An agency that tries to stabilize international currency exchange rates and lend to countries having difficulty in financing their international transactions.

M1, M2 – Measures of the money supply. M1 is the money that can be used directly for transactions money, while M2 (also called "broad money") is M1 plus savings accounts and other "near monies."

Real business cycle – The idea that business cycles fluctuate according to rational expectations and enjoy complete price and wage flexibility.

Recession – The conventional definition is a drop in aggregate output for two successive quarters or more.

Stagflation – When inflation and high unemployment occur together during a recession.

Tragedy of commons – The idea that things that are owned collectively by a group are not efficiently used or maintained because individuals do not bear the full cost of their actions. The name comes from a problem in England in the 1700s, when some land was held in common for the community. Individual farmers had an incentive to overgraze common land to benefit their own animals, but overall the community suffered because of the damage to the land; no one had an incentive to care for the land.

PROTECTIONISM VERSUS FREE TRADE

The argument for free trade is essentially that each country should specialize in producing the goods and service in which it has a comparative advantage. If a trade barrier is imposed on imports, demand may drop as consumers have to pay a higher price, and the country's production is less efficient. Trade has potential benefits for all nations. Goods are not usually imported unless their net price is below that of their domestic alternative. Two countries that sell to each other in this way will benefit people in both nations, enabling them to consume more goods while spending less.

The benefit of free trade is one of the few matters that most economists agree upon. In practice, however, companies, industries, and whole sections of society, together with the politicians who represent them, often demand that their special interests should be protected from foreign competition. A major drawback of protectionist measures is the danger of retaliation – for instance, in 1980 when the UK imposed controls on imports of clothing from Indonesia (worth about £10mn), Indonesia canceled a defense order worth £40mn and reconsidered other UK import deals worth £350mn.

Another objection is that economic efficiency, meaning producing things that people want at the lowest possible cost, is often ignored in protectionist arguments.

Nevertheless, there are sometimes grounds for selective protectionist measures.

» Protecting jobs – foreign competition may cost local people their jobs. Although these workers may be ultimately employed in other industries that are expanding, there is a cost. People may have to move to another part of the country to get work, and spend time and money acquiring new skills. Those who are in the weakest position and find it difficult to change may suffer hardship for many years.

» Unfair trade practices from foreign competitors – while anti-trust laws in the US prevent companies from monopolizing an industry and engaging in "predatory" pricing, other countries, notably Japan, have no such restrictions. In such cases, free trade clearly does not mean the same thing to all trading partners. Many American economists regard this as a legitimate argument for protection, especially in the face of a powerful industry in a foreign country behaving "strategically" in international trade. "Dumping" goods in other countries at a price that is lower than the real production cost is often seen as unfair, for instance by the US and the European Community in relation to certain Japanese exports.

» Cheap foreign labor is unfair – developed nations tend to have a higher cost of living and pay higher wages than developing countries. Manufacturers in high wage countries, for instance, may claim that it is unfair that their competitors in, say, China, are able to produce goods at a fraction of their own costs because of low wages.

» National defense and avoiding dependence on other nations – in the event of war, it may not be possible to import some products and services from other nations. For instance, steel is regarded as essential for national defense in the US. Any industry seeking protection, however, tends to use the national defense argument, so a question remains over which industries are truly essential to national defense.

Weaker countries often argue that becoming over-reliant on a larger trading partner for essential goods leads to the loss of political independence; some protectionists claim that the superpowers consciously create dependence in their small trading partners.

» Safeguarding new industries – an industry that is just beginning in a country may have the potential to develop a major competitive advantage as it matures. Protection may legitimately be needed from larger foreign industries to keep it alive in the early stages. However, protecting a young industry that can never become efficient is a waste of resources (labor, capital, and raw materials) that could be better used (see Chapter 6, Peruvian car manufacturing).

JOHN MAYNARD KEYNES (1883–1946)

Much of macroeconomics is based on the work of the British economist John Maynard Keynes, whose 1936 book, *The General Theory of Employment, Interest and Money*, attempted to explain the problems of the interwar slump in Britain and the Great Depression. Hitherto, prices and wages were thought to be the key determinants of employment levels, but Keynes argued that aggregate demand for goods and services and aggregate expenditure were actually the most important factors and that governments should stimulate aggregate demand during recessions (see Chapter 3). According to Keynes, the government's duty is to act as employer of last resort during recessions by, for example, spending on large public projects, even if this causes a government deficit. Keynes was also the first person to emphasize the links between the money markets and goods markets.

The Roosevelt New Deal of the thirties was the first attempt to apply Keynesian ideas to the problems of recession. Following WW2, many countries took up the idea of government intervention with enthusiasm, and "Keynesian" economics came to mean active government participation in the economy at all times. Keynes, in fact, was against the high taxation levels required by a permanently large public sector, but during post-war reconstruction the political arguments for state involvement in production, such as the nationalization of industries, became popular, particularly in Europe. The US, too, adopted aspects of Keynesianism, believing that the state could successfully "fine tune" the economy to stabilize production output and employment levels.

The recession of the 1970s and 80s revealed problems with this approach and there is now a general feeling that the neo-Keynesian methods were not precise enough instruments to control an economy, particularly during prosperous periods. Keynes himself, a polymath intellectual with a penchant for currency speculation, might well have been horrified to see the way his ideas were applied after his death, although he would no doubt have applauded the general increase in living standards that has been achieved in developed countries since the Second World War.

MONETARISM AND MILTON FRIEDMAN

Monetarism emerged as a response to the perceived ineffectiveness of state intervention during the 1970s and 80s. To understand its proposals, we need to examine the concept of the velocity of money.

Suppose A purchases goods from B for $100 in January. B may hold the money until April before spending it with C, who holds it until July when she spends it with D, who doesn't spend the $100 until December. The $100 has changed hands four times during the year, so its "velocity" is 4.

In the real world, GDP is used (imperfectly) as a substitute for the total value of transactions in an economy. The velocity of money is calculated as the ratio of nominal GDP to the money supply. If the total value of finished goods and services produced in one year is $9trn and the money supply is $1trn, the velocity of money is 9/1 = 9.

The quantity theory of money assumes that the velocity of money remains virtually constant over time. If this is true, then changes in the supply (stock) of money will be equal to changes in nominal GDP and the demand for money does not depend on interest rates.

Monetarism is not a monolithic ideology, and there is little general agreement amongst monetarists on definitions, let alone on how its principles should be applied. Almost everyone, including non-monetarists, agrees that prolonged inflation is a purely monetary phenomenon. In other words, inflation cannot go on indefinitely unless there is an increase in the money supply, which is controlled or at least strongly influenced by a nation's central bank.

Monetarist guru Milton Friedman (see Chapter 9) believes that central banks should restrict themselves to keeping the money supply growing in line with real output growth.

SUPPLY-SIDE ECONOMICS

The stagflation of the 1970s gave rise to the idea that the real problem was that too much taxation and regulation was reducing incentives to work, invest and save. The solution was therefore to stimulate supply rather than demand, which had been the main focus of orthodox approaches. Tax cuts would encourage both individuals and companies to spend and invest, while lower regulations would help businesses to grow. This would lead to an increase in the supply of labor, since more people would want to work, or work harder, and there would be more capital available for investment. Both inflation and unemployment would fall.

The Laffer Curve (see Fig. 8.1) illustrates the argument for reducing taxation.

According to Laffer, if the tax rate is 0%, then people will want to work, but the government will receive no tax revenues. If the tax rate is 100%, no one will want to work because all their income will go to the government, so the government will still receive no revenues. Since the curve is symmetrical, there are pairs of points (one on the upper part of the curve and one on the lower, for instance A and B in Figure 8.1) where tax revenues to the government will be equal, but the lower part of the curve will relate to a higher supply of labor than the upper part because the tax rate will be lower.

The "Reaganomics" of the 1980s brought in substantial tax cuts in 1981 in an attempt to set rates on the lower part of the curve. The US economy promptly came out of recession, inflation fell, and,

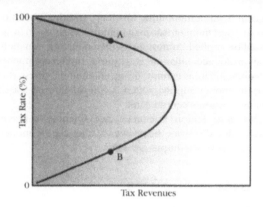

Fig. 8.1 The Laffer Curve – a depiction of the idea that the size of the total tax revenues varies with both the level of taxation and the consequent level of willingness to work.

except for one year, tax revenues rose throughout the 1980s. Was this a vindication of supply-side economics?

Some people think not. The reduction in inflation may have been a delayed effect of the recession of 1980 and 1981. Tax cuts may encourage people to feel that their financial needs are being met more easily, so they can afford to work less rather than more – in fact, some studies in the 1980s found that the increase in labor supply was quite small in the US.

Reaganomics claimed that the government could increase expenditure despite the tax cuts and still balance the budget. This did not occur; the US government deficit increased by almost $2trn between 1983 and 1992.

The recovery that began in 1982 might be accounted for by the effect that supply-side measures had on demand, and also because the Fed increased the money supply by 20% between 1981 and 1983 and interest rates dropped dramatically.

ALAN GREENSPAN

Alan Greenspan is the chairman of the Federal Reserve Board (the Fed), the central bank of the USA. Most famous for his 1996 remark about the possibility of "irrational exuberance" forcing stock market valuations to unsustainably high levels, this soft-spoken Republican occasionally attracts criticism for his cautious approach to managing US monetary policy.

Greenspan first held public office under Nixon as director of policy research in the late 1960s, and became chairman of the Fed in 1987, a post he will hold until 2004. The fact that he has presided over the Fed during four presidencies is a testament to his political as well as economic shrewdness. His power to influence the US economy through short-term interest rates has made him the focus of attention worldwide, leading him to choose his words carefully when making public statements. His measured, calming approach has been applauded by business people and politicians of all hues, although some object to his view that financial markets should, as far as possible, be left to respond to economic developments freely.

Greenspan believes (see Chapter 4) that the severe corporate downsizing of the 1980s and early 1990s have helped to dampen demands for wage increases, thus keeping inflation low. The Fed, therefore, has been able to afford to ease up on monetary restraints since then. A strong advocate of deficit reduction, Greenspan has presided over a period when the US deficit dropped, almost reaching zero in 1997.

Alan Greenspan is a firm believer in the most conservative of all virtues, saving. Throughout the stock market boom of the late 1990s, he frequently aired his concerns that people were spending their stock market gains because they regarded them as permanent increases to their wealth. "We save too little," he complains, arguing that domestic investment still largely depends on domestic saving. The recent stock market collapse lends credence to his views.

THE PRODUCTIVITY PROBLEM AND GROWTH

The New Economy argument (see Chapter 4) has largely been based on the view that new high-tech businesses have found a way to increase productivity in the US. To put this into context, we need to recall the great productivity debate of the late 1970s and early 1980s. US productivity has gradually declined since the 1960s, as it has done in other developed countries.

Explanations for this vary, including the low rate of US saving, less investment in R&D, investment diversion to energy saving, and increased regulation. Much discussion revolved around the apparent success of Japan compared with the US. By the 1990s, however, Japan's growth had dramatically slowed and attention shifted elsewhere. Various long-term growth policies were attempted in the US from the 1960s onwards that attempted to increase savings, stimulate investment generally, encourage R&D, reduce regulations, and improve education.

MEASURING PRODUCTIVITY

As we saw in Chapter 4, official productivity figures are not thought to be accurate. This is because it is very difficult to measure the effects of many products. For instance, it is easy enough to measure the number of new PCs made, but it is much harder to accurately measure the increased benefits each new model, with its increased memory and other features, gives to their users – a lawyer might save weeks of preparation by using a PC to research cases on the Internet, and book production times have been drastically cut through IT, yet this kind of saving of time is not measured by the official data. Many economists argue that this problem has been true since the late nineteenth century, and applies equally, if not more so, to indirect productivity advances brought about by trains, cars, airplanes, telephones, and so on.

There is little agreement over why the overall trend seems to be one of declining productivity growth in most developed nations but it is clear that there are political difficulties in adopting a sustained long-term growth policy in a democracy. Such policies are likely to take many years before they produce impressive results and may be expensive in the mean time, making them vulnerable to criticism. Without general support, politicians are likely to drop such policies in favor of measures that engender short-term popularity.

There is not even a consensus that growth itself is a good thing. Supporters of growth say that growth produces all kinds of desirable benefits including better health, longer life expectancy, more choice in many areas of life, more and better goods – in short, a better quality of life for all. Anti-growth arguments focus on four main points.

1 Growth may actually reduce quality of life – many lifestyles, such as that of small farmers, become uneconomic as a country grows, and some people regret their passing. Environmental damage, stress-filled urban lives, pollution, and hazardous waste are just a few examples of the undesirable effects of industrial growth. Many things that have an effect on the quality of life cannot be traded and may disappear because of growth – simple pleasures may be lost to generations devoted to an economic rat race.

2 Growth encourages inequity – the rich save more than the poor, and these savings are available for investment, a source of growth. Critics of growth say that the have-nots in society are locked out of many of the benefits afforded by growth, yet must endure the worst of the undesirable effects.

3 Growth will use up the world's resources – in the 1970s there was much debate about this, stimulated by a group called the Club of Rome that predicted dire consequences from continued growth. Since the 1970s, governments and corporations have become more sensitive to this issue; new resources have been found, more efficient technologies developed and conservation measures have been taken. Most if not all major corporations now try to take an "eco-friendly" public relations position. As well as the predictors of doom, there are also moderates who point to the rapid growth in the developing world as a problem. In this view, the developing world may run out of resources by the time they mature enough to need them for internal consumption.

4 Growth creates artificial dependency – traditionally, consumers are seen as "sovereign" in their desires, and markets merely supply what is wanted. Some growth critics argue that sophisticated marketing and consumer credit manipulate consumers into becoming perpetually indebted purchasers of useless items.

Sustained economic growth clearly implies trade-offs with what might be called "well-being" and different nations find different compromises between the two. Not many people in developed countries would want growth at any price, but they may have the luxury of choices that most people in LDCs do not enjoy. In poorer countries, needs are often so basic and urgent that such a debate can seem irrelevant.

PAUL ROMER: NEW GROWTH THEORY

Paul M. Romer, a Professor of Economics at Stanford University, is a leading developer of "new growth theory," which attempts to explain the dynamics of wealth creation better. He argues that while classical economic theory is good at explaining how extracting natural resources works, it does not properly explain the "information economy." Extracting natural resources such as oil from the earth is subject to diminishing returns: as more oil is produced, there is less of it left and extraction becomes more expensive. In the case of computer software or biotechnology, however, there are large initial development costs, but the costs of subsequent production are very small. For example, once you have designed a bacterium to produce a desired product – say, insulin – there is almost no limit to the amount you can produce.

Classical economics sees labor and capital as the two inputs that increase productivity (output) – to increase production, you either employ more workers or invest in better machinery. Romer argues that technology and knowledge are also "inputs" – new designs and techniques can also increase productivity. In high-tech industries, productivity has massively increased for decades while prices have declined, the opposite of what happens with finite resource extraction. The more we invent and discover, the better we get at the process of discovery, so our ability to create growth and value builds on itself, says Romer.

Romer thinks that having an economy conducive to having and applying ideas may be more important than having resources or capital. Japan lacked resources and capital, for instance, but has achieved astounding growth over the last 50 years. Romer comments:

> "The lesson from the Japanese experience is clear: mundane forms of applied research, such as design work or product and process engineering, can have large cumulative benefits for the firm that undertakes them and even larger benefits for society as a whole. Moreover, the gains from applied research are largest not when it

is dictated by government agency priorities or academic interests, but instead when it is closely integrated into the operations of a firm and motivated by the problems and opportunities that the firm faces."

On this view, the hope for LDCs lies in investing in education and providing incentives to its people to acquire ideas from other parts of the world, create their own, and apply those ideas commercially. Effective patent and copyright protection, for instance, are powerful incentives to the creation and transmission of ideas. Many LDCs have suffered a "brain drain" as local talent has emigrated to the developed world where there is more opportunity for fulfilling "knowledge work."

Romer delights and offends both ardent free marketeers and protectionists with his fresh approach. For example his views on what he calls "meta-ideas," ideas about how to encourage the creation and distribution of useful ideas, suggest that developed nations should find new institutions to support "a high level of applied, commercially-relevant research in the private sector. These institutions must not impose high efficiency costs and, most important, must not be vulnerable to capture by narrow interests." This implies a combination of state intervention with private enterprise.

Although still young (he is in his early 40s), Romer is widely tipped for a Nobel Prize in economics, although skeptics say that more work is needed on how to apply his theories. Intellectually rigorous and cautious, Romer is nevertheless willing to make a firm prediction – that the leading country in the twenty-first century will be the one that finds a new and more effective way (a "meta-idea") of supporting private sector production of commercially applicable ideas. Romer is certain that such ways will be found.

Resources

A look at some important books relating to the development of today's business environment. Useful Websites and further reading.

» Big business in the economy
» Monetarism
» International trade
» Technology and growth
» Internet resources
» Further reading.

"All models are wrong but some are useful."

George Box

This chapter contains a basic guide to some of the key Websites and books to consult when beginning to get to grips with the global economy.

Macroeconomic issues are easier to understand in hindsight; the problem with topical coverage is that it tends to address unanswerable questions about the future. For this reason, most of the books discussed in detail here were written some time ago. Nevertheless, most of them are classics and provide a valuable perspective on current debates. With issues that are complex and difficult to understand, novelty is not always a virtue – appreciating how we got here is an important part of judging where we are likely to go next.

BIG BUSINESS IN THE ECONOMY

The Visible Hand: The Managerial Revolution in American Business

This Pulitzer Prize winning book by Alfred D. Chandler Jr. analyzes how large corporations developed to their current importance. He argues that recognizably modern businesses developed when administrative co-ordination began to be more effective than market mechanisms in enhancing productivity and lowering costs, giving rise to a management hierarchy. Management hierarchies came to be self-perpetuating, expansionist, and increasingly professionalized. As a separation between management and ownership developed, management professionals tended to focus on long-term stability and growth rather than short-term gains, and corporations grew larger, reaching their position of whole branches of today's economy. Written in 1977, this book provides a good background to today's issues regarding the globalization of business.

» Chandler, A.D. Jr. (1977) *The Visible Hand: The Managerial Revolution in American Business*. Harvard Belknap, Cambridge, MA.

The Myth of the Global Corporation

This 1999 book argues against the common view that multinationals are more influential in the global economy than governments, and that they are so "transnational" as to owe no allegiance to any nation. The authors describe US, German, and Japanese firms in particular, showing that MNCs from these countries tend to pursue national objectives and operate very different systems. For instance, MNCs from different countries vary widely in the importance they give shareholders, in their closeness to banks, in management accountability, and in their exposure to international capital markets. A potential strain between national ideas about corporate governance and global pressures for standardization is discussed. Power is not shifting from governments to supranational corporations, say the authors, but the tendency for states to pursue nationalist policies in trade, technology, and finance could well bring about the eventual disintegration of the global economy.

» Doremus, P.N., Keller, W.W., Pauly, L.W., Reich, S. (1999) *The Myth of the Global Corporation*. Princeton University Press, Princeton.

MONETARISM

A Monetary History of the United States, 1867–1960

Arch-monetarist Milton Friedman and co-author Anna Jacobson Schwartz's 1963 book had a major impact on economic thinking in the US, and is still one of the most frequently quoted texts in economics. Prior to its publication, it was generally thought that having a government monetary policy was ineffective and that the state should restrict itself to keeping interest rates low enough to keep unemployment at an acceptable level. Friedman established that the quantity of money is controllable and strongly influences the economy.

The book covers the Great Depression in much detail, arguing that a better monetary policy could have greatly reduced the problems it caused, notably at a crucial point in 1930/31 when a banking crisis developed.

The book is accessible and highly readable, without equations in the main text – it is probably the best foundation for an understanding of the genuine theoretical advances that monetarism has produced. Money does not explain everything, nor does Friedman claim so; the point is that the flow and quantity of money has important, and to some degree manageable, effects on the economy.

» Friedman, M. & Schwartz, A.J. (1963) *A Monetary History of the United States, 1867-1960*. Princeton University Press (for the National Bureau of Economic Research), Princeton.

INTERNATIONAL TRADE

Mercantilism

Controversial when it was first published in 1931 because of fears of fascism, this book proposes that the success of the West over the last 500 years has been in large part due to mercantilism, a way of organizing labor, business, and government to work for national prosperity by promoting overseas trade. Pure laissez-faire is impossible, it suggests. Overseas trade was the most effective way of generating taxable revenues, increasing the strength of the state and thereby benefiting the whole country, and from the 1500s to the 1700s, mercantilist policies helped to build wealthy nation states out of chaotic feudalism. In the nineteenth century, powerful European nations continued to follow mercantilist policies, dominating the rest of the world both economically and politically.

The twentieth century rise of competing ideologies that give greater weight to labor (socialism, communism) or business (capitalism) than to government made this book seem irrelevant, although much of its historical analysis was generally accepted by critics. Today's globalization process has brought a changing and uncertain relationship between the three economic elements (labor, business, and government) and has revived interest in the book as people look for new ways of organizing countries to create prosperity.

» Heckscher, E.F. (1931) *Mercantilism*. George Allen and Unwin, London. Revised, second edition, edited by Ernst F. Söderlund, 1955, 2 volumes. (Originally published as *Merkantilisment: Ett led i den ekonomiska politikens historia*. P.A. Norstedt and Söner, Stockholm.)

TECHNOLOGY AND GROWTH

The Unbound Prometheus: Technological Change and Industrial Development in Western Europe from 1750 to the Present

This classic work sheds much light on the newness or otherwise of the New Economy debate. The author, David Landes, believes that the principal engine for development in Western Europe during the last 250 years has been technological advance, although he also examines the important role of natural resources. In the latter part of the book he focuses on wider macroeconomic issues after WW1, but continues his argument that knowledge is portable and public, and that business willingness to take the risks to acquire new knowledge was a key factor in growth. He examines a multitude of industries in great detail to see whether this idea applies. Much food for thought on the reasons why the efficiency gains of today's information industries take so long to show up in overall productivity rates.

» Landes, D.S. (1969) *The Unbound Prometheus: Technological Change and Industrial Development in Western Europe from 1750 to the Present*. Cambridge University Press, Cambridge MA.

INTERNET RESOURCES
US Federal government
» http://www.census.gov/ *Census Data*: Population statistics – US Census Bureau.
» http://www.bls.gov/fls/ *International Labor Statistics*: Bureau of Labor Statistics' site.
» http://www.cbo.gov/ *The Congressional Budget Office*: Source for information on the finances and programs of the US federal government.
» http://www.cbpp.org/ *Center on Budget and Policy Priorities*: US Federal government budget figures.

Economists
» http://www.wws.princeton.edu/pkrugman/ *Paul Krugman*: A page established and maintained by economist Paul Krugman to give interested parties easy access to some of his more recent writings.
» http://www.stanford.edu/promer/ *Paul Romer*: Romer was the lead developer of "new growth theory."

Statistical data
» http://www.economagic.com/ *Economic Time Series Page*: Economagic has a database of over 100,000 economic time series. This is a useful site for basic information on trends.

» http://www.geohive.com/index.html *GeoHive*: Statistics on the human population.

» http://www.amstat.org/publications/jbes/index.html *Journal of Business & Economic Statistics*: The Journal of Business and Economic Statistics (JBES) publishes articles dealing with a broad range of applied problems in business and economic statistics.

News magazines

» http://www.economist.com/ *The Economist (of London)*: One of the world's best news magazines. News articles on global issues. On-line articles on a variety of topics affecting economies across the world.

» http://www.findarticles.com/ *FindArticles.com*: FindArticles.com is a large archive of published articles that you can search for free. It contains articles dating back to 1998 from more than 300 magazines and journals.

General economics

» http://www.nber.org/ *National Bureau of Economic Research*: Nearly 500 NBER Working Papers are published each year, and many subsequently appear in scholarly journals. Papers are available in PDF format and the list is updated weekly.

» http://www.aeaweb.org/jep/ *Journal of Economic Perspectives*: The Journal of Economic Perspectives (JEP) attempts to fill a gap between the general interest press and most other academic economics journals.

» http://www.awlonline.com/parkin/econ100/ *Michael Parkin*: At this Website, you'll find a rich array of "learning tools" to boost your understanding of economics.

» http://www.eh.net/ *Economic History Resources*: Created in 1993, they provide several free electronic discussion lists to provide resources and promote communication among scholars and students in business history, economic history, the history of economics, and related fields.

» http://fic.wharton.upenn.edu/fic/wfic/papers.html *Wharton School of Finance*: The Wharton Financial Institutions Center provides access to its many opinions and "meaningful insights" through the site.

Internet

» http://www.icannwatch.org/ *ICANN Watch*: ICANN Watch reports on decisions and events at ICANN (The Internet Corporation for Assigned Names and Numbers). The policies and decisions of this organization affect how the Internet is governed. The site offers commentary and criticism from a wide variety of sources, guided only by the belief in the power of ideas and informed discussion and debate to shape events and institutions.

» http://www.law.miami.edu/ *Michael Froomkin's Home Page*: Michael Froomkin is a frequent contributor to ICANN Watch. Here you will find additional articles and information on the Internet, the economy and law topics.

Market-oriented

» http://www.msdw.com/gef/ *Stephen Roach at Morgan Stanley*: Market-oriented articles on recent economic news.

Non-government organizations (NGOs)

» http://www.worldbank.org/research/growth *World Bank Economic Growth*: The research branch of the World Bank tries to pull together the relevant information about economic growth. This area lists recent research and project reports.

» http://www-wds.worldbank.org/ *World Development Sources*: World Development Sources (WDS) is a Web-based text search and retrieval system which contains a collection of World Bank reports most of which are scanned. Also included is the ASCII text of the report generated from the image by OCR.

» http://www.imf.org/ *International Monetary Fund*: IMF maintains an extensive list of reports for countries and regions on-line. Many of the older papers are available for download in PDF format. Current papers require payment.

» http://www.oecd.org/ *OECD*: Organization for Economic Co-operation and Development Publications and its statistics. Covers economic and social issues from macroeconomics, to trade, education, development, and science and innovation.

» http://www.un.org/ *United Nations*: The United Nations sponsors many programs for social, political, and economic development. The reports of these and other activities are available at this site.

» http://www.wto.org/ *World Trade Organization/*: The WTO Website contains material for a range of users, from the general public to students, academics, and trade specialists. It includes introductions to WTO activities and a large database of official documents.

» http://www.wtowatch.org/ *WTO Watch/*: WTO Watch places copies of news and WTO publications on their site. Sponsored by the Institute for Agriculture and Trade Policy.

Regional trade and economic centers

» http://www.mac.doc.gov/nafta/ *North American Free Trade Agreement*: One of the primary objectives of the Office of NAFTA and Inter-American Affairs (ONIA) is to increase access to foreign markets for US exports, through the elimination of tariff and non-tariff barriers to trade. This site provides access to documents and reports.

» http://www.aseansec.org/ *Association of South East Asian Nations*: The site provides many links to historical and cultural information and directories of businesses in the region.

» http://www.apecsec.org.sg/ *Asia Pacific Economic Cooperation*: A group of 21 nations of the Pacific Rim. The site includes all of the official statements from APEC ministers, economic reports on each nation, tariffs, intellectual rights, and maintains a virtual library of all APEC meetings.

» http://europa.eu.int/ *European Union*: Official site of the European Union.

FURTHER READING

Agmon, T., Hawkins, R.G. & Levich, R.M. (eds) (1984) *The Future of the International Monetary System*. Lexington Books, Lexington, MA.

Aliber, R. (1987) *The International Money Game*, 5th edn. Basic Books, New York.

Amihud, Y. & Levich, R. (eds) (1994) *Exchange Rates and Corporate Performance*. Irwin, Burr Ridge, Ill.

Bergsten, C.F. & Graham, E.M. (1995) *The Globalization of Industry and National Governments*. Institute for International Economics, Washington.

Brewer, T. (1985) *Political Risks in International Business*. Praeger, New York.

Buckley, A. (1992) *Multinational Finance*, 2nd edn. Prentice Hall, New York.

Chacoliades, M. (1970) "Increasing returns and the theory of comparative advantage." *Southern Economic Journal.*

Coffey, P. (1987) *The European Monetary System, Past, Present and Future*, 2nd edn. Kluwer Academic Publishers, Dordrecht, Netherlands.

Dennett, D. (1995) *Darwin's Dangerous Idea: Evolution and the Meanings of Life*. Simon and Schuster, New York.

Dunning, J.H. (1993) *The Globalization of Business*. Routledge, London.

Elfstrom, G. (1991) *Moral Issues and Multinational Corporations*. St. Martin's Press, New York.

Fallows, J. (1995) *Looking at the Sun*. Pantheon, New York.

Fleming, J.M. (1955) "External Economies and the Doctrine of Balanced Growth." *Economic Journal*, **June.**

Fujita, M., Krugman, P. & Venables, A. (1999) *The spatial economy*. MIT Press, Cambridge.

Fukao, M. (1995) *Financial Integration, Corporate Governance and Performance of Multinational Companies*. Brookings, Washington.

Greider, W. (1996) *One World, Ready or Not*. Simon and Schuster, New York.

Grossman, G.M. & Rogoff, K. (eds) (1995-) *Handbook of International Economics , Vol.*3. Elsevier Science, Amsterdam.

Helpman, E. & Krugman, P. (1985) *Market Structure and Foreign Trade*. MIT Press, Cambridge.

Hirschman, A. (1958) *The Strategy of Economic Development*. Yale University Press, New Haven, Conn.

Krugman, P. (1991) "Increasing returns and economic geography." *Journal of Political Economy.*

Krugman, P., (1994) "Does Third World growth hurt First World prosperity?" *Harvard Business Review*, **July.**

Krugman, P. (1995) *Development, Geography, and Economic Theory*. MIT Press, Cambridge.

Krugman, P. (1996) "How to be a crazy economist." In: S. Medema and W. Samuels (eds) *Foundations of Research in Economics: How do Economists do Economics?* Edward Elgar, Brookfield, Vermont.

Krugman, P. & Obstfeld, M. (1994) *International Economics: Theory and Policy*, 3rd edn. HarperCollins, New York.

Lall, S. *et al.* (1983) *The New Multinationals*. Wiley, New York.

Leibenstein, H. (1957) *Economic Backwardness and Economic Growth*. Wiley, New York.

Lewis, W.A. (1954) Economic Development with Unlimited Supplies of Labor. *The Manchester School*, 22.

Lewis, W.A. (1955) *The Theory of Economic Growth*. Allen and Unwin, London.

Little, I., Scitovsky, T. & Scott, M. (1970) *Industry and Trade in Some Developing Countries*. Oxford University Press, Oxford.

Milner, H. (1988) *Resisting Protectionism*. Princeton University Press, Princeton.

Myrdal, G. (1957) *Economic Theory and Under-developed Regions*. Duckworth, London.

Nelson, R. (1956) "A Theory of the Low Level Equilibrium Trap in Underdeveloped Economies." *American Economic Review*, **May.**

Ohlin, B. (1933) *Interregional and International Trade*. Harvard University Press, Cambridge.

Oxelheim, L. (1993) *The Global Race for Foreign Direct Investment: Prospects for the Future*. Springer-Verlag, Berlin.

Penrose, R. (1989) *The Emperor's New Mind*. Oxford, New York.

Porter, M. (1990) *The Competitive Advantage of Nations*. Free Press, New York.

Romer, P, (1991) "Increasing Returns and New Development in the Theory of Growth." In: W. Barnett *et al.* (eds) *Equilibrium Theory and Applications: Proceedings of the 6th International Symposium in Economic Theory and Econometrics*.

Rosenberg, N. (1982) *Inside the Black Box: Technology and Economics*. Cambridge University Press, Cambridge.

Scitovsky, T. (1954) "Two Concepts of External Economies." *Journal of Political Economy*, 144–51.

Smith, R.C. & Ingo, W. (1990) *Global Financial Services*. Harper and Row, New York.

Utriu, R. (1996) *Troubled Industries*. Cornell University Press, Ithaca.

Wells, L. (1983) *Third World Multinationals*. MIT Press, Cambridge.

Yoffie, D. (ed.) (1995) *Beyond Free Trade*. Harvard Business School Press, Boston.

Yoshino, M. & Rangan, U.S. (1995) *Strategic Alliances*. Harvard Business School Press, Boston.

Ten Steps to Making Global Finance Work

This chapter presents some of the key opportunities, techniques, and survival strategy in the global economy, including:

» new markets in the developing world
» Europe
» accessing capital markets
» managing forex risk versus speculation
» Foreign Direct Investment (FDI) and the alternatives.

''Achieving free trade is like getting to heaven. Everyone wants to get there, but not too soon.''

Anonymous

1. NEW MARKETS IN THE DEVELOPING WORLD

As we have seen, the recipe for future prosperity in the developing world is complex and controversial. Nevertheless, the globalization process has opened up certain countries, promising a substantial long-term boost to world growth and creating opportunities for companies to expand out of their own maturing markets.

OPPORTUNITY IN CHINA

Until 1979 China was a closed economy. Since then, it has modernized rapidly, largely because of its massively improved trade and investment relations with the rest of the world.

By 2020, China could displace Japan to become the largest trading nation in the world after the US, potentially generating substantial growth both for itself and its trading partners. Progress depends on factors such as joining the WTO (with a consequent further reduction in trade barriers) and sustaining foreign investment by major reforms in its financial system. In the face of problems, foreign investment can disappear as quickly as it arrives, so China's rulers face a major challenge in macroeconomic management in the medium term.

The World Bank estimates that by 2020, China's market share of the world export market for clothing will reduce as it moves up the value chain into light manufacturing and transport, machinery, and equipment. Exports from North America, Europe, and Japan to China are expected to rise by 6.5% annually until 2020, mainly in knowledge- and capital-intensive goods and services, but also in food, where North America has a comparative advantage. China's growth, therefore, is expected to benefit the developed nations. While South-East Asian countries are fearful that China will undercut them in many industries, they are likely to enjoy net gains overall, according to the World Bank.

2. COPING WITH RECESSIONS

The conventional definition of a recession is a period when aggregate output declines for two consecutive quarters. They occur quite frequently – the US, for instance, experienced seven recessions in addition to the Great Depression during the twentieth century. They do not necessarily occur in tandem around the world. It is reasonable to assume that they will continue to occur periodically, so any business must have a strategy for recession survival. Some economists argue that recessions are good for the economy because they drive inefficient firms out of business and force all firms to cut waste and use their resources better. Acting quickly to cut costs is likely to be effective once it is clear that that a recession is underway; assuming that growth will be permanently uninterrupted is likely to be fatal.

OIL PRICES AND THE GLOBAL ECONOMY

When OPEC raised oil prices in the 1970s it caused chaos in many economies that led to stagflation and a considerable transfer of wealth from oil-consuming to oil-producing nations. Could it happen again?

In the late 1990s, there was concern that oil prices had roughly tripled in less than two years, but it is unlikely that the global economy will be affected as severely as it was in the 1970s. For one thing, there was a sharp price drop in 1977 and most of the subsequent price increases were simply a return to previous levels. More importantly, the world learned from its mistakes; the developed countries have shifted substantially towards less energy-intensive technologies and use oil much more efficiently. Even large price hikes in oil are unlikely to affect their economies seriously. Developing countries, however, are intense energy users and are much more vulnerable.

Much depends on the strategy of the oil exporters, many of whom have fiscal and current account deficits and have been postponing infrastructure projects. If they spend the money gained from increased oil prices on these projects, it will be recycled back to the rest of the world rather than being stored as foreign currency reserves, as it was in the 1970s.

3. MANAGING PEOPLE IN THE KNOWLEDGE ECONOMY

While no one knows whether knowledge-based industries will permanently boost GDP growth in the rich countries, they are replacing manufacturing as the most important businesses. Management guru Peter Drucker believes that knowledge will soon become the key resource in the developed world. With an aging but healthy population, rich countries will expect people to work an extra ten years, into their seventies, he says.

Not everyone will be a winner, even amongst knowledge workers themselves. While some people may prosper as independent consultants or on short-term contracts, others are likely to find the expected move away from full-time, job-for-life employment difficult. "Knowledge technicians," highly educated workers in areas such as IT, medical laboratories, and engineering, may not be particularly well paid. They are predicted to become the fastest growing group, replacing the skilled manual workers of today in numbers and, possibly, negotiating power.

This has important implications for human resource management. How will companies keep their knowledge workers? Recently in the US the trend has been to offer stock options and earnings-related bonuses. Drucker claims that this "always fails" and suggests that a better way will be:

» to allow greater autonomy in making decisions;
» to take an inclusive approach to company goals and strategy;
» to ensure that people are given appropriate tasks; and
» to provide continuous training

4. EUROPE

As the world's largest trading bloc, with 40% of world trade, the European Union cannot be ignored. It represents a substantially different form of capitalism to the US model and although stock market capitalism has helped to galvanize many EU firms, a complete adoption of the "Anglo-Saxon" business norm is unlikely.

The EU's reason for existence is primarily strategic, to provide security and prosperity both within its own borders and in the countries to the east. Plans for enlargement have aroused little opposition in the rest of the world, perhaps, some say, because the EU is unlikely to become united enough to project political power as a single entity, but is seen as a positive force for prosperity and growth.

Protectionist policies are common within the EU, between member states (despite regulations to the contrary) as well as with the outside world. EU firms are trying to streamline themselves, but tough labor protection laws are likely to hamper efficiency. US-style peremptory firing of staff is unacceptable.

The diversity of Europe's members means that different countries want different things out of the union. For example, some countries like Britain and Denmark have so far stayed out of the single currency. Enlargement will add to the pressures against tighter federalization. One solution that may emerge is that the EU becomes a collection of overlapping deals between member states, where some choose to co-operate together closely on certain issues while opting out of others. Markets may continue to become freer in Europe, but they are unlikely ever to approach a pure state of laissez-faire, even internally.

5. GLOBALIZATION AND THE WTO

Globalization is not as far advanced as many people seem to think. The world is only very partially integrated. The GATT/WTO process, aimed at lowering trade barriers around the world in order to raise economic growth, has achieved much but has taken more than half a century to do so. The vocal anti-globalization backlash has got it wrong in so far as it claims that globalization hurts the poor; it actually helps them, and most developing nations want freer trade.

Businesses need to be aware of changing public attitudes, and today most large companies emphasize their commitment to values such as environmentalism, consumer protection, and energy conservation. Faced with the tough disclosure rules for public companies, "green" legislation and consumers' power to influence politicians, companies are paying more than lip service to these values – many companies publish detailed information on their efforts to reduce waste of raw materials, for instance.

Globalization may be good for business generally, but is it good for your business? Some firms might prefer to enjoy a monopoly rather than struggle with competitors in a fast changing world. New markets, freer trade, and capital flows only offer opportunities to companies that are efficient, flexible, and innovative.

6. ACCESSING CAPITAL MARKETS

Entrepreneurs dream of successfully floating their companies on a major stock market. Not only will it make them, the prior owners, rich, but it also offers a very large supply of capital for growth. A small private business may be dynamic and have many opportunities to expand, but it cannot sell corporate bonds (a fixed rate loan) easily or issue shares to the general public. It must seek finance from banks, venture capitalists, or private investors, which limits the amount it can borrow and is more expensive. Even large firms in countries with "segmented" capital markets suffer from this problem.

Going public on a major market is not easy. The firm must usually have a good track record, although recently the rules have been relaxed for certain dynamic industries, such as IT and biotechnology, to allow the flotation of start-ups.

To access the global capital markets, a company needs to:

» establish and maintain good relations with institutional investors and, eventually, the public;
» conform to very exacting standards of information disclosure, which is costly; and
» consider starting slowly by issuing corporate bonds to create and encourage investor confidence.

7. MANAGING FOREX RISK

The world's currency system is broadly one of "managed floating" driven by market forces. Many countries' currencies, however, are traded in extremely thin and highly regulated markets, throwing doubt on the official rate of exchange. It is sometimes very difficult for a company even to obtain a quotation for these currencies from forex dealers.

If your company does business in a foreign country, it is exposed to three main exchange rate risks.

» *Transaction risk*: the chance that the exchange rate changes after you have bought or supplied goods and services at an agreed price. This also applies to lending and borrowing abroad.

» *Operating risk*: your business in a foreign country may be going well, but if there is a crisis (such as the Asian currency crisis of 1997), it will negatively affect your expected future cash flows there. One way to mitigate this is to borrow money in that currency and use your sales income to service the debt – this is called ''natural hedging.'' There are many variations on this approach, such as ''back to back'' loans, where two companies in different countries lend each other equal amounts in their own currency to be repaid at the same time.

» *Accounting risk*: US listed companies, for instance, must restate their foreign subsidiaries' accounts in US dollars when preparing their group financial statements. There is a risk that a change in the exchange rate could affect the parent's published figures. A ''balance sheet'' hedge avoids this by balancing foreign currency assets and liabilities. You can almost never have a balance sheet hedge and a hedge against transaction risk at the same time; faced with a choice, managers tend to prefer to hedge against transaction risk (real cash losses).

Managing forex exposure is a specialized field. A long run of gains in forex dealing can tempt companies to think of their forex managers as a profit center. Continuous selective hedging is essentially increasing risk through speculation rather than trying to reduce it. Firms rarely admit this.

8. FOREIGN DIRECT INVESTMENT (FDI)

If your firm wants to invest abroad, it must have a competitive advantage in its home market, such as management expertise, economies of scale, financial strength, differentiated products, or better technology. The advantage must be specific to your firm and it should be transferable to the foreign market.

Before embarking on an FDI, defined as creating a wholly- or partly-owned foreign subsidiary, consider the other options, which may be less risky.

» *Exporting*: Selling to foreign agents and distributors. The least risky, but least profitable, method.
» *A strategic alliance*: Many EU firms are swapping shares and entering into joint ventures with other European companies as a way of pooling resources and protecting themselves against competitors.
» *Licensing and management contracts*: Licensing technology or ''lending'' managers to a foreign firm.

FDI is a much more risky and expensive option. It should only be undertaken where the potential rewards outweigh the risks – for example, if your company will dominate the foreign market.

9. VALUING FOREIGN ACQUISITIONS

Buying a foreign company is often a better way of entering a foreign market than starting from scratch. It is quicker, eliminates some local competition (they're working for you now), and companies are sometimes available at bargain prices.

As with all acquisitions, the great danger is in paying too much. Buying a foreign firm in a developing country is likely to be costly in terms of due diligence, and the likely actions of the host government need to be fully understood. The acquiring company also needs to be sensitive to how it is perceived by local people. Don't assume that US-style market capitalism works the same way in developing nations.

10. MNC INTERNATIONAL PORTFOLIOS

Investment theory tells us that you can reduce risk by diversifying across several investments in different sectors. This idea can be applied to MNCs too, because the returns on operations in different countries vary and do not normally fluctuate in tandem. In other words, when some countries are doing poorly, other countries may be doing well, although there appears to be a trend towards closer correlation of returns.

Calculating the optimal weighting of the "portfolio" of an MNC's businesses is abstruse and based on assumptions that may not prove to be accurate. It can, however, be a useful way of looking at an MNC's overall strategy to answer questions like: "Suppose risks suddenly increase in China – should we reduce our investments there and increase them in Brazil? How might that affect our overall returns?"

KEY LEARNING POINTS

1 Countries are opening up their markets around the world. China and India, with their vast populations, are predicted to become major trading nations by 2020. Look for ways to take advantage of these new opportunities.

2 In the 1990s excitement about the booming tech stocks led some companies to behave as if recessions were a thing of the past. Don't make that mistake – make sure you have a plan of action in place to respond effectively to downturns.

3 "Knowledge workers" are different from the skilled manufacturing workers of the past. They are more mobile and require more autonomy, training, and participation in strategy. Is your company winning the loyalty of its knowledge workers?

4 If your firm is in Europe, it may have trouble seeing the wood for the trees. Freer trade and the prospect of enlargement are creating great uncertainty. Take the trouble to research the issues and try to gain an overall perspective on trends.

5 The anti-globalization movement is a sign of the power of consumers. Are your company's policies in line with the attitudes of people in your markets? Are you publicizing and explaining your policies in a way that people can understand?

6 Is your firm taking full advantage of the global capital markets? Investors in different countries perceive risks differently – you may need to look abroad for the cheapest capital in the amount you require.

7 Foreign trade implies forex risk. Is your company claiming to reduce the risks by hedging while actually increasing them?

8 FDI is the most costly and riskiest method of foreign trade, but offers the most rewards in some cases. FDI only works if you have a transferable competitive advantage. Most firms start out by exporting before making heavier commitments.

9 Buying a foreign firm can be the cheapest and most cost-effective way of direct investment into a foreign market (FDI). Make sure you don't pay too much and that you fully understand how the host government will behave. How will you get local customers on your side?

10 MNCs are judged by their consolidated returns, which may fluctuate if they are overly reliant on particular markets. International portfolio theory is a way of looking at all the MNC's businesses to see if their relative weighting can be adjusted to reduce the fluctuation in the overall return. This might be done, for instance, by postponing further expansion in certain countries in favor of projects in others.

Frequently Asked Questions (FAQs)

Q1: What are GATT and the WTO?

A: See Chapter 3, The General Agreement on Tariffs and Trade (GATT) and the World Trade Organization (WTO).

Q2: Why is the theory of comparative advantage central to free trade?

A: See Chapter 2, The theory of comparative advantage.

Q3: Is growth always good?

A: See Chapter 8, The productivity problem and growth.

Q4: When could protecting an industry be justified?

A: See Chapter 8, Protectionism versus free trade.

Q5: What's new about the New Economy?

A: See Chapter 4, Is there really a New Economy?

Q6: Is it true that the biggest multinationals have larger sales than most countries' GDPs?

A: See Chapter 5.

Q7: Why should multinationals care what consumer pressure groups think?

A: See Chapter 7, Nestlé – global corporate responsibility.

Q8: What's really happening in the EU?

A: See Chapter 7, The European Union: restructuring business.

Q9: What was "Reaganomics" all about? Did it work?

A: See Chapter 8, Supply-side economics.

Q10: How can my business take advantage of globalization?

A: See Chapter 10.

Index

Printed and bound by CPI Group (UK) Ltd, Croydon, CR0 4YY

13/04/2025

14656559-0004